Our Lady at Fátima: Prophecies of Tragedy or Hope?

Antonio A. Borelli • John R. Spann

With a special Foreword by
Plinio Corrêa de Oliveira

Our Lady at Fátima: Prophecies of Tragedy or Hope?

The Apparitions and the Message of Fátima in Accordance with the Manuscripts of Sister Lúcia

The American Society for the Defense of Tradition, Family and Property wishes to express its gratitude to Dr. Antonio Augusto Borelli for his permission to publish this sixth edition of his book on Our Lady of Fatima, first published in the monthly *Catolicismo* of July 1975. This work, now published in numerous editions worldwide, has attained a circulation of over three million copies. About 95% of the total appeared in book or booklet form, the rest being published in magazines or newpapers.

The countries of publication and the respective number of copies are:

Argentina	54,500	Italy	60,000
Australia	11,000	Paraguay	5,000
Austria	2,500	Peru	25,000
Bolivia	24,000	Philippines	5,000
Brazil	1,700,500	Poland	21,000
Canada	23,000	Portugal	202,500
Chile	23,500	South Africa	15,000
Colombia	35,000	Spain	47,000
Costa Rica	20,000	United States	127,500
Ecuador	47,000	Uruguay	13,000
France	560,000	Venezuela	23,000
Germany	500	Total	3,045,000

The languages in which it has appeared and the respective number of copies are:

English	153,000	Polish	39,000
French	85,000	Portuguese	1,908,000
German	3,000	Rumanian	2,000
Italian	60,000	Russian	310,000
Latvian	10,000	Spanish	325,000
Lithuanian	100,000	Ukranian	50,000
		Total	3,045,000

Sixth American edition
© 1996 by the American Society for the Defense of
Tradition, Family and Property
First American edition 1975; second American edition 1985; third American
edition 1994; fourth American edition 1995; fifth American edition 1996;
sixth American edition 1996.

**The American Society for the Defense
of Tradition, Family and Property**
P.O. Box 1868
York, Pennsylvania 17405
Tel. (717) 225-7147
Fax (717) 225-7382

ISBN # **1-877905-28-3**
Library of Congress Catalog Card Number **94-073143**
Printed in Canada

Printed in Canada

Contents

Chapter III

Chapter IV

Bibliography

Foreword
by
Plinio Corrêa de Oliveira

The Timeliness
of the
Message of Fátima

Plinio Corrêa de Oliveira

Plinio Corrêa de Oliveira was born in Sao Paulo, Brazil, in 1908. From a young age he had an intimate and tender devotion to Our Blessed Mother that profoundly molded every aspect of his life.

He graduated from the School of Law of the University of Sao Paulo. As a young man, he distinguished himself as an outstanding Catholic speaker and journalist, and was particularly active in the Marian Congregation.

Prof. Corrêa de Oliveira played a key role in organizing the Catholic Electoral League and was elected to the Constitutional Convention of 1934 with the largest number of votes. He was the youngest congressman in Brazil's history.

He was a professor at the University of Sao Paulo Law School College and later held the chair of History at the Pontifical Catholic University of Sao Paulo.

The Archdicesian Board of Catholic Action of Sao Paulo elected him as their first president. He was also director of the Catholic weekly Legionario. Numerous Brazilian newspapers carried his articles, and countless readers from around the world benefited from his 14 books.

As a devoted Catholic, his pen and word were always at the service of the Catholic Church and Christian civilization. In 1960, he founded the Brazilian Society for the Defense of Tradition, Family and Property which he directed until 1995. His exemplary life and brilliant literary works inspired the foundation of similar associations in 25 countries across the globe.

Tireless in urging constant recourse to Our Lady, he never lost a chance to win for her another devotee. On countless occasions, when asked for advice, he would repeat his favorite saying: "Have more devotion to Our Lady!"

Prof. Plinio Corrêa de Oliveira passed away on October 3, 1995. He was widely known as a champion of Our Blessed Mother and authored many gripping articles linking current events to Her call to conversion at Fatima.

Copies of his life story, published in the United States, in both the Catholic and secular press, are available by writing to the address below.

The American TFP - P.O. Box 1868 - York, PA 17405

The Timeliness of the Message of Fátima

The message of Fátima comes to the fore today—three quarters of a century after the famous apparitions of Our Lady in Portugal in 1917—with renewed interest, to the point that it was accorded extensive coverage not long ago (September 27, 1991) on the front page of *The Wall Street Journal.*

An impressive coincidence of two events that marked the century

What was it that gave the revelations of Fátima this unexpected vitality?

A nation that occupies a central place in today's global political scene was deeply involved in them.

The coincidence of two events—the revelations of Fátima and the Russian revolution—is very noticeable, as both occurred during the same year, 1917. Communism seized power in Russia exactly 25 days after Our Lady's last apparition at Fátima. A message transmitted to the three seers—the little shepherds Lúcia, Francisco, and Jacinta—and which remained secret until 1942, pointed to the "errors of Russia" as the focus of serious disturbances, which have truly been shaking the whole world for the greater part of the century. That same message predicts the eventual conversion of that nation.

Under these conditions, the spectacular fall of the Berlin Wall and the Iron Curtain on November 9, 1989, with the political upheavals that preceded and followed it in the countries of Eastern Europe, could not but be associated with the predictions of Fátima. Could not those events be signs that Our Lady is fulfilling Her promises?

The Wall Street Journal article points precisely to this.

It is impossible to make an all-inclusive study of that fundamental point of the international political situation within the narrow confines of a foreword. We must nevertheless make at least a brief summary of it as we present a book containing the essentials of the Fátima message.

A reproach to the world, a threat of punishment, a promise of peace

What does the average reader derive from the Fátima message after giving sufficiently serious attention to it?

Such a reader draws from the message the extremely serious fact that Our Lady reproaches the world for certain sins and threatens it with definite punishments should Her requests not be heeded. The conditional character of the promises of Fátima appears thus perfectly configured. That is, Our Lady leaves humankind an escape from the coming chastisement through amendment of life.

Along these lines, the expiatory character of the requests made by Our Lady are outstanding: the Communion of Reparation of the first Saturdays of five consecutive months, followed by the consecration of Russia to the Immaculate Heart of Mary. If these requests were to be fulfilled, Russia would be converted and would abandon its errors, and a basic factor of world disturbance would be deactivated. The world would enjoy peace again, the peace of Christ in the Reign of Mary.

The moral crisis in the West has done nothing but increase

We ask: Did the faults, the sins cease? Was the expiation made? Was the consecration of Russia performed according to the exact terms established by Our Lady?

We answer: To begin with the more evident element, the moral crisis in the West did nothing but increase rapidly. Fashions degenerated, approaching ever more generalized nudity. The dreadful instability of marriage, the acceptance of homosexuality as normal, the number of apostasies among the clergy and the ranks of religious orders of both sexes for reasons having much to do with the lack of regard for the vow of chastity, abortion, the co-education of boys and girls, sex-education in the schools, all of the methods of birth control, all are symptoms of the deterioration affecting ever wider sectors of Western society.

The atheistic sect of communism tried to construct a society without God

A society from which the idea of God has been virtually banished was constructed in the Eastern countries under the control of the atheistic communist sect. From the highest point of the State to the smallest details of each individual life, everything was organized in opposition to the Natural Law, as codified in the Ten Commandments of the Law of God. Communist legislation abolished private property, instituted the most complete egalitarianism, and practically extinguished the family, making marriage a matter of mere public registry that legally insignificant formalities can change at the good pleasure of the episodically joined couples.

Reform of morality, the great oversight

Thus, among so many reforms that everyone deems necessary— either in the West or in the East—no one pleads for a solution to that which most offended Our Lady, that is, the decline of morality, whether private or public, by restoration of the institution of the family, with the strengthening of the indissolubility and sacrality of marriage, of parental authority over the children; freeing children from the abusive intervention of the secular if not directly atheistic State, and so on and so forth.

The requests of Our Lady were not heeded in a fundamental point

Consequently, without entering into the controversy of whether or not the successive Papal consecrations of the world to the Immaculate Heart of Mary have fulfilled the conditions established by Our Lady for the conversion of Russia (the nation that must be specifically mentioned in the formula of consecration), any statement about the promises of Fátima being fulfilled would demand the greatest circumspection, considering that men have not corresponded to the requests of Our Lady in a fundamental point, that is, the amendment of life.

Nixon's advice to prez: Forget family values

ppealing to prejudice
ld be

1917

THE BETTMANN ARCHIVE

An Average American Family

Teen sex a pregnancy

Many U.S. teenagers
rejecting advice to ref
sex. Some of the result

Percent of adolescent
(age 15-19) sexually a

60   59
46%
30   51
27%
0   White
70 75 Blac

DISAPPEARING DA

Unwed couples beginning to gain cities' recognition

22,000 babies abandoned'

WASHINGTON – A
study has fo
22,000 babies
tals each

Study Says for Unwed Women

1994

Never-married parents increasing

Children living with divorced parents
Children living with never-married parents

50%
40%
30%
20%
10%
1986 1987 1988 1989 1990 1991

Census study says 'nuclear' family waning

Birthrat Up 7

By ELIZABETH SHOGREN
Los Angeles Times

WASHINGTON — The
conventional model of Ameri-

as one where both biological
parents are present and all
children were born after the
marriage. It excludes house-
holds with single or divorced

Boy can sue to

Perestroika, from hope to thorns

However, the fact is that the Gorbachevian promise of establishing *perestroika* in Russia produced—inside and outside that country—what may be one of history's greatest geopolitical earthquakes. Nations kept under the iron glove of Soviet communism without descrying the least hope of liberation, suddenly shook off that yoke and took their own destiny in hand. Germany, cut in two from top to bottom, reunited. How can we fail to view such encouraging transformations with hope?

After the first moments of optimism, however, realistic observers began to detect thorns on the stems of the roses. Seventy years of communism in Russia and almost half a century in the satellite or annexed nations devastated the institutions and generated an apathy in the peoples that shows no signs of a quick recovery. On the contrary, the analysts and the world media have begun to emphasize with ever more frequency the very serious possibility of migrations from those nations—speaking sometimes of tens of millions—of hungry people searching for means of survival in the West. In the face of this potential new "invasion of barbarians," the Western nations are concerned that if it reaches the foreseen proportions, it will produce unimaginable devastations. Beside the economic impoverishment, the mixing of such disparate ethnic groups will cause those nations to lose their identities. The West, which did not resist well the doctrines of communism, would see itself destroyed by an apparently a-ideological operation.

At this point, an unavoidable question poses itself: When Gorbachev decided on the fall of the Iron Curtain, was this not exactly the effect he had in mind? It is understandable that many Europeans have begun to long for the Iron Curtain, formerly viewed as the horror wall but now seeming to be a protective barrier...

Retreat or metamorphosis of communism?

The most careful minds always mistrusted *perestroika,* fearing it would contain a vile trick of communism in its belly. Today, public opinion in the West is slowly discovering that the true aim of *perestroika* was really obscure. Perhaps the day is not far off when the questionable authenticity of communism's retreat will reveal itself as nothing but a metamorphosis and that from the altered caterpillar the "pretty" butterfly of self-management will emerge, the self-management that all the theoreticians and supreme leaders of communism, from Marx and Engels to Gorbachev, always presented as the extreme and perfect version of communism, its quintessence. In the preamble of the Soviet constitution, this was stated in all its details. Communism, apparently overthrown, would have spread its errors over all the world.

In this, the prophecies of Fátima would be confirmed, for they warned: If men do not amend their lives, Russia will spread its errors throughout the world!

Clarity, vigilance, and courage

It is thus important, and very much so, to know the Message of Fátima in its authentic version, as it is found in the manuscripts of Sister Lúcia, of which the reader has a clear and objective synthesis in the present book.

The American Society for the Defense of Tradition, Family and Property offers it to the public with certainty that it will benefit those who would lucidly, vigilantly, and courageously face the prospective extraordinary events that may occur, thrusting humanity into perplexity and affliction.

For those who have faith, the words of Our Lady in Fátima will always resound in their ears: "In the end, my Immaculate Heart will triumph".

What Happened at Fátima

Antonio A. Borelli

NOSSA SENHORA DE FÁTIMA,
QUANDO NA IRIA POISOU,
A REZAR PELAS ALMINHAS
A PORTUGAL ENSINOU."

Antonio A. Borelli Machado

The author was professor of moral philosophy in the Department of Economics, Accounting, and Insurance of Sacred Heart College in Sao Paulo. Graduating as a civil engineer from the Polytechnic School of the University of Sao Paulo, he worked in that profession for fifteen years. Following that, he has dedicated his time entirely to the Brazilian Society for the Defense of Tradition, Family and Property, TFP. He is presently the director of the TFP's Comission of Readers, its department for research and documentation, which analyzes, summarizes, and catalogues more than four hundred periodicals in thirteen languages from twenty-five countries and which maintains a specialized library on current doctrinal subjects.

He is a contributor to the prestigious monthly cultural magazine *Catolicismo*, which circulates throughout Brazil. He has most distinguished himself as the author of the book *The Apparitions and Message of Fátima, According to the Manuscripts of Sister Lúcia*, a thoroughly documented and incisive study of the revelations of Mary Most Holy to the three little shepherds Lúcia, Jacinta, and Francisco in Cova da Iria in 1917, a study that has been of great interest to scholars and the great public.

Introduction

In books about Fátima, the narration of the apparitions and the conversations of Our Lady with the seers are usually not the primary focus; instead these are intermixed with other related events and aspects of the story, such as the local repercussions of the apparitions, the interrogations of the seers and witnesses, the cures and extraordinary conversions that followed, the fascinating details of the spiritual progress of the privileged children, and numerous associated episodes. All of this is perfectly natural and understandable.

Nevertheless, after reading these books, many feel a desire for a text that would devote special attention to the contents of the apparitions. They seek to more fully grasp the meaning of the message Our Lady came to communicate to men and thus heed her admonitions.

To satisfy this legitimate desire, we have attempted to put together a story centered around what occurred between the Virgin and the seers and between the Angel of Portugal and the seers. The numerous edifying and picturesque facts interwoven with the story of Fátima have been set aside in order to focus attention on this essential part.

The accounts of the apparitions of the angel in 1916 and Our Lady in 1917 are followed by private revelations received by the seers, especially Sister Lúcia. Since they complement the apparitions at Cova da Iria, they could not be omitted here.

The first edition of this work was based primarily on two well-known works, which we recommend to those who are anxious to read more about the story of Fátima. One is William Thomas Walsh's *Our Lady of Fátima*; the other, *Era uma Senhora mais brilhante que o sol* by Father John M. de Marchi, I.M.C. (See bibliography.)

Father De Marchi spent several years in Fátima, questioning witnesses of the events and carefully recording their remarks. He interviewed Sister Lúcia and was able to examine her manuscripts, which we shall discuss further on.

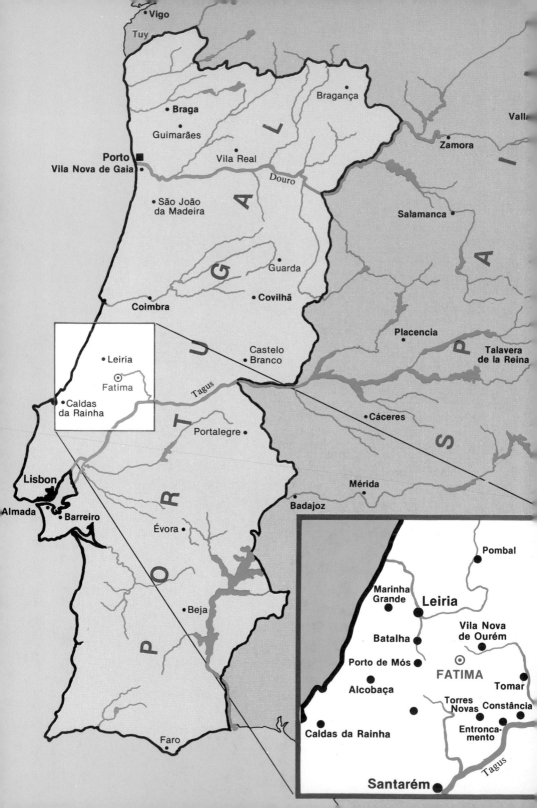

In 1946, William Thomas Walsh also went to Portugal to interview witnesses and do research. He spoke with Sister Lúcia and relied extensively on her four memoirs in the writing of his book.

The works of Father De Marchi and Walsh are well-researched and in essential agreement in most details. Nevertheless, in our 1967 edition of this book, further care was taken to compare them with books of other authors, who complete and clarify certain facts and details. Unfortunately, it was then impossible to examine the authoritative sources themselves, the manuscripts of Sister Lúcia. Those manuscripts had not yet been published, save for a few excerpts reproduced by several authors who had been able to examine them.

When the 1967 edition was first published on the occasion of the fiftieth anniversary of the apparitions, we expressed the desire to see the complete text of those precious manuscripts brought to light for the edification of all those who are devoted to Our Lady of Fátima. Today it behooves us to acknowledge the fulfillment of this desire. The manuscripts were at last published in 1973 by Father Antonio Maria Martins, S.J. in *Memórias e Cartas da Irmã Lúcia*.

However, we are still eagerly awaiting a work that, in addition to the memoirs and letters already published, contains all the interrogations to which Sister Lúcia was subjected,[1] the documents of the canonical

---

1. In his book *A Vidente de Fátima dialoga e responde pelas Aparições*, Father Sebastião Martins dos Reis presents (a) the successive interrogations of the seers made by the Visconde de Montelo at the time of the apparitions (Visconde de Montelo was the pseudonym of Canon Manuel Nunes Formigão of the patriarchal see of Lisbon); (b) the interrogation made by Father H.I. Iongen, a Dutch Montfortist who visited with Sister Lúcia on February 3 and 4, 1946, and published an account of these interviews in the May, July, and October, 1946, issues of the bimonthly review *Mediatrice et Reine*; (c) the identification of the historic places of Fátima by the seer on May 20, 1946; (d) the interrogation by Dr. J.J. Goulven, which was answered in writing by Sister Lúcia on June 30, 1946 (Father Sebastião Martins dos Reis relates that Sister Lúcia sent the manuscript to the bishop of Leiria, who in turn ordered that it be typewritten and that three copies be made. After being signed by the seer, one of the copies was sent to Dr. Goulven, another remained with the seer, and the third was filed with the original by order of the bishop of Leiria. The author does not specify whether he transcribed the document from the manuscript or one of the copies.); and (e) the interrogation by Father José Pedro da Silva (later bishop of Viseu), answered by the seer on August 1, 1947.

Besides these testimonies and the aforementioned interviews granted to Father De Marchi and Mr. Walsh, Sister Lúcia granted another interview over a period of five

e escoras de animais espantosos e desconhecidos, mas transparentes como negros carvões em braza. Assustados e como que a pedir socorro levantámos a vista para Nossa Senhora que nos disse com bondade e tristeza: Vistes o inferno, para onde vão as almas dos pobres pecadores; para as salvar Deus quer estabelecer no mundo a devoção a Meu Imaculado Coração, se fizerem o que eu vos disser salvar-se-ão muitas almas e terão paz: a guerra vai acabar: mas se não deixarem de ofender a Deus, no reinado de Pio XI começará outra peor. Quando virdes uma noite alumiada por uma luz desconhecida, sabei que é o grande sinal que Deus vos dá de que vai a punir o mundo de seus crimes, por meio da guerra, da fome e de perseguições à Igreja e ao Santo Padre.

Para a impedir, virei pedir a consagração da Russia a Meu Imaculado Coração, e a comunhão reparadora nos primeiros sábados. Se atenderem a meus pedidos a Russia se converterá e terão paz: se não, espalhará seus erros pelo mundo, promovendo guerras e perseguições à Igreja, os bons serão martirizados, o Santo Padre terá muito que sofrer, varias nações serão aniquiladas: por fim o Meu Imaculado Coração triunfará. O Santo Padre consagrar-me-á a Russia que se converterá e será concedido ao mundo algum tempo de paz. Em Portugal se conservará sempre o dogma da fé etc. Isto não o digais a ninguém. A Francisco sim, podeis dizê-lo.

Quando rezais o terço, dizei depois de cada mistério: Ó meu Jesus perdoai-nos, livrai-nos do fogo do inferno, levai as alminhas todas para

**The end of Sister Lúcia's account of the
second part of the secret in Memoir IV**

investigation,[2] and all the seer's correspondence that still exists.[3] The importance of the Fátima message certainly warrants such a meritorious effort.

The four accounts Sister Lúcia wrote are usually designated as Memoirs I, II, III, and IV. (The remaining parts of Father Antonio Maria Martins' book are referred to here simply as Memoirs.)

Memoir I is a collection of Sister Lúcia's reminiscences for a biography of Jacinta. On September 12, 1935, the mortal remains of the little seer of Fátima, who died in 1920, were exhumed. Her face was found

---

days (September 16 through 20, 1935) to the writer Antero de Figueiredo. The seer comments on this interview in her own writings. (See Memoir IV, pp. 368-376.)

2. After eight years of thorough inquiry, the canonical process of investigation concluded in favor of the apparitions. In a pastoral letter dated October 13, 1930, the Most Reverend José Alves Correia da Silva, bishop of Leiria, declared: "In virtue of the considerations set forth, and others which for the sake of brevity we omit, humbly invoking the divine Holy Ghost and trusting in the protection of Mary Most Holy, and after hearing the reverend advisers of this our diocese, we hereby (1) declare the visions the children had at Cova da Iria, parish of Fátima, of this diocese, on the thirteenth day of the months of May to October, worthy of belief; and (2) officially permit the cult of Our Lady of Fátima." (See Rendeiro, pp. 179-180.)

3. In *Memórias e Cartas da Irmã Lúcia*, Father Antonio Maria Martins, S.J. includes letters from the seer to her confessor, Father José Bernardo Gonçalves, S.J., and points out that it was Father Gonçalves who "later became responsible for the seer's most valuable correspondence.

"Most of these letters deal with matters of conscience. That is why they cannot be published now." (See Memoirs, p. 399.)

On page xx of the book's preface, Father Martins says that besides the memoirs, the writings of the seer include "thousands of letters, most of them written after her admission to the Carmel of Saint Teresa in Coimbra, on March 25, 1948."

In a letter to Father Gonçalves of January 21, 1940, Sister Lúcia tells about the censorship her correspondence underwent and how this prevented or made it difficult for her to discuss matters of conscience with him. She says: "I have wanted to write Your Reverence for a long time, but several reasons have impeded it, the main one being censorship. To write while not being able to say what I had to seemed to me a waste of your time; to write it under censorship was impossible. At times the necessity was not small, but (we must have) patience. All has passed, and Our Lord has taken care of everything. As He has sent the wound, so has He sent the cure. He knows very well that He is the only doctor on earth. In fact, I must confess I also doubted that Your Reverence would be willing to waste time on me. So I thank Your Reverence immensely for the letter and for the charity Your Reverence has practiced with me in opening my way. May Our Lord reward Your Reverence." (See Memoirs, p. 418.)

Jacinta and Francisco's home

Lúcia's home

to be incorrupt. The Most Reverend José Alves Correia da Silva, bishop of Leiria, sent Sister Lúcia a photograph taken on this occasion. In her letter of thanks, she referred to the virtues of her cousin. The prelate then ordered her to write all she knew about the life of Jacinta. Thus, the task of writing the first manuscript began. It was finished around Christmas 1935.

In April of 1937, Father Ayres da Fonseca told the bishop of Leiria that Sister Lúcia's first account suggested the existence of yet unknown facts related to the apparitions. This prompted a new order from the bishop for Sister Lúcia to write the story of her life, a task she accomplished between November 7 and 21 of the same year. In this account she also speaks, although very briefly, of the apparitions of Our Lady and, for the first time, officially discloses the apparitions of the Angel of Portugal. Until then, she had remained silent about them for several reasons: She had been advised to do so by the archpriest of Olival, Father Faustino José Jacinto Ferreira (to whom she had narrated the apparitions), later reinforced by the same recommendation from the bishop of Leiria; additionally, the criticism and mockery resulting from her account of the three apparitions of the angel in the spring and summer of 1915 and the severe reprimands of her mother always prompted her to great caution and discretion. But Sister Lúcia's great reluctance to talk about herself and, therefore, about the apparitions in her memoirs still mystifies the reader.

In 1941, the bishop of Leiria again ordered the seer to provide, to the best of her ability, a detailed narrative of Jacinta's life for a book being written by Canon José Galamba de Oliveira about the youngest seer. "This order," writes Sister Lúcia, "touched the depth of my soul like a beam of light telling me that the time had come to reveal the first two parts of the secret...." (See Memoirs, p. 444.) Thus, Sister Lúcia began her third manuscript by revealing the currently known parts of the secret of Fátima. Following this, she recorded the impression these revelations had made on Jacinta. This account is dated August 31, 1941.

Surprised by such revelations, Canon Galamba de Oliveira concluded that Sister Lúcia had not told everything in her previous accounts and urged the bishop of Leiria to command her to write the complete story of the apparitions. "Your Excellency...give her the order to write everything, and I mean everything. She will have to wander a while in purgatory for staying silent about so many things." Sister Lúcia excused herself, saying that she always acted out of obedience. Canon Galamba de Oliveira insisted that the bishop order her "to tell everything, everything; she should hide nothing." (He was apparently alluding to the third part of the secret.) The bishop, however, chose not to become involved. "That I shall not order. In secret matters, I shall not meddle." Instead, he simply told the seer to make a complete narration of the apparitions. (See Memoir IV, pp. 314, 316. The underscoring is Sister Lúcia's own.) Then she wrote the fourth manuscript, which bears the date of December 8, 1941. In this memoir, Sister Lúcia, for the first time gave a systematic and ordered account of the apparitions, stating in the conclusion of the narrative that nothing of all that she could remember had been "knowingly" omitted, save, evidently, the third part of the secret, which she had not been ordered to reveal. (See Memoir IV, p. 352.)

In the 1967 edition of this work, we tried to reconstruct the development of the apparitions with the greatest possible fidelity, using the principal bibliographical sources then available. Unfortunately, discrepancies among the best authors were found. Many doubts were settled with the publication of the manuscripts of Sister Lúcia, but some still linger. Accordingly, a consultation with the surviving seer is still desirable so that she may clarify the ambiguities wherever possible.

To satisfy the reader's desire to know the Fátima message in all its authenticity, we have revised the original version of this work, integrating the manuscripts of Sister Lúcia. The dialogues reproduce her very words verbatim. Since the authors consulted for the former version proved to have been generally faithful to the manuscripts, nothing substantial in the original edition has been changed.

In offering this work to the American public, we hope to contribute toward making the message of Our Lady of Fátima more widely known, loved, and observed.

Chapter I

The Apparitions of the Angel of Portugal

Before the apparitions of Our Lady occurred, Lúcia de Jesus dos Santos and her cousins, Francisco and Jacinta Marto, who all lived in the village of Aljustrel in the township of Fátima, had three visions of the Angel of Portugal, also called the Angel of Peace.

The First Apparition of the Angel

The angel first appeared either in the spring or summer of 1916 at Loca do Cabeço, a rocky outcrop near the top of a knoll called Cabeço, not far from Aljustrel. This is Sister Lúcia's account of the apparition:

"We had been playing for a while when a strong wind shook the trees. Since it was a calm day, this made us raise our eyes to see what was happening. Then we began to see, well above the trees that covered the stretch of land to the east, a light whiter than snow in the shape of a transparent young man who was more brilliant than a crystal struck by the rays of the sun.

"As he approached, we began to see his features. He was a young man of great beauty about fourteen or fifteen years old. We were surprised and ecstatic. We did not utter a word.

"Once he drew near us, he said: 'Fear not. I am the Angel of Peace. Pray with me.'

"Kneeling down, he bowed forward until his forehead touched the ground. We imitated him, led by a supernatural inspiration, and repeated the words we heard him say: 'My God, I believe, I adore, I hope, and I love Thee. I beg Thee forgiveness for those who do not believe, do not adore, do not hope, and do not love Thee.'

"After he had repeated this twice, he rose and said: 'Pray thus. The Hearts of Jesus and Mary are attentive to the voice of your supplications.'

"Then he disappeared.

"The supernatural atmosphere that enveloped us was so intense that we were almost unaware of our own existence. For a long time, we remained in the same position we were in when he left, repeating the same prayer. The presence of God was so intense and intimate that we dared not speak to each other. On the following day, we felt our spirits still enveloped in that atmosphere, which was but slowly disappearing.

"None of us thought of talking about this apparition or of recommending secrecy, for the incident itself demanded it. It was so intimate that it was difficult to utter a word about it. This might well have been the apparition that impressed us the most, because it was the first one thus manifested." (See Memoir II, pp. 114, 116, and IV, pp. 318, 320; De Marchi, pp. 51-52; Walsh, pp. 39-40; Ayres da Fonseca, p. 121; Galamba de Oliveira, pp. 52-57.)

The Second Apparition of the Angel

The second apparition occurred in the summer of 1916 over the well at the house of Lúcia's parents, next to which the three children were playing. This is how Sister Lúcia narrates what the angel said to them:

"'What are you doing? Pray! Pray a great deal! The Sacred Hearts of Jesus and Mary have merciful designs concerning you. Offer prayers and sacrifices constantly to the Most High!'

"'How must we sacrifice?' I asked.

"'Offer God a sacrifice of anything you can as an act of reparation for the sins with which He is offended and as a supplication for the conversion of sinners. Draw peace upon your country by doing this. I am its guardian angel—the Angel of Portugal. Above all, accept and endure with submission whatever suffering the Lord sends you.'

"Then he disappeared.

"The angel's words were impressed upon our souls like a light that made us understand who God is, how much He loves us and wishes to be loved, the value of sacrifice and how it pleases God, and how He converts sinners because of it." (See Memoir II, p. 116, and IV, pp. 320,

"Fear not. I am the Angel of Peace. Pray with me."

322; De Marchi, p. 53; Walsh, p. 42; Ayres da Fonseca, pp. 121-122; Galamba de Oliveira, pp. 57-58.)

The Third Apparition of the Angel

The third apparition occurred either at the end of the summer or the beginning of the autumn of 1916, once again at Loca do Cabeço. According to Sister Lúcia's account, it took place as follows:

"As soon as we arrived there, we began to say the angel's prayer on our knees, with our faces to the ground. 'My God, I believe, I adore, I hope, and I love Thee....' I do not know how many times we had said this prayer when we saw an unknown light shining over our heads. We rose to see what was happening, and we saw the angel bearing a chalice in his left hand. Drops of blood fell into the chalice from a Host suspended over it. Leaving the chalice and the Host suspended in the air, the angel prostrated himself beside us and said the following prayer three times:

"'Most Holy Trinity, Father, Son, and Holy Ghost, I adore Thee profoundly and offer Thee the most precious Body, Blood, Soul, and Divinity of Jesus Christ, present in all the tabernacles of the earth, in reparation for the insults, sacrileges, and indifference with which He is offended. And through the infinite merits of His Most Sacred Heart and of the Immaculate Heart of Mary, I beg Thee for the conversion of poor sinners.'

"After this, rising up, he again took the chalice and the Host in his hand; he gave the Host to me and the contents of the chalice to Jacinta and Francisco to drink, saying: 'Take and drink the Body and Blood of Jesus Christ, who is horribly insulted by ungrateful men. Make reparation for their crimes and console your God.'

"He again prostrated himself on the ground and repeated with us the same prayer three more times. 'Most Holy Trinity....'

"Then he disappeared.

"Compelled by the supernatural force that enveloped us, we imitated the angel in everything, that is, prostrating ourselves as he did and repeating the prayers he said. The strength of God's presence was so intense that it absorbed and annihilated us almost completely. It seemed to deprive us even of the use of our bodily senses for a long period of time. For several days afterward, we performed our physical actions as though sustained by that same supernatural being who compelled us to do them. The peace and happiness we felt were great, but intimate, as our souls were entirely concentrated on God. The physical weariness that overwhelmed us was also great.

"I do not know why, but the fact is that the apparitions of Our Lady had a very different effect on us. There was the same intimate gladness, the same peace and happiness. But instead of physical weariness, we felt a certain expansive liveliness, a sense of glee instead of that annihilation in the Divine Presence, a certain communicative enthusiasm instead of that difficulty in speaking. But, in spite of these feelings, I felt the inspiration to remain silent, especially about certain things. In the interrogations, I felt an intimate inspiration that suggested to me the answers, which, although true, would not disclose what I should still keep secret." (See Memoir II, p. 118, and IV, pp. 322-326; De Marchi, pp. 54-55; Walsh, pp. 43-44; Ayres da Fonseca, pp. 122-123; Galamba de Oliveira, pp. 58-59.)

The apparitions of the angel in 1916 were preceded by three other visions from April to October of 1915, in which Lúcia and three other little shepherd girls (Maria Rosa Matias, Teresa Matias, and Maria Justino) saw something suspended in the air over the trees in the valley. It was "a kind of cloud whiter than snow, somewhat transparent, with a human form...a figure like a statue made of snow that the rays of the sun had turned somewhat transparent." This description is the one given by Sister Lúcia herself. (See Memoir II, p. 110, and IV, pp. 316, 318; De Marchi, pp. 50-51; Walsh, pp. 27-28; Ayres da Fonseca, p. 119; Galamba de Oliveira, p. 51.)

May 13, 1917

Chapter II

The Apparitions of
the Blessed Virgin

At the time of the apparitions of Our Lady, Lúcia de Jesus, Francisco, and Jacinta were, respectively, ten, nine, and seven years old, having been born March 22, 1907, June 11, 1908, and March 11, 1910. As we have said, the three children lived in Aljustrel, a hamlet of the township of Fátima. The apparitions took place on a small property belonging to Lúcia's parents called Cova da Iria, about a mile and a half from Fátima on the road to Leiria. Our Lady appeared over a holm oak just over three feet high. Francisco could only see Our Lady; he could not hear her. Jacinta could see and hear her. Lúcia could see, hear, and talk with the Blessed Virgin. The apparitions occurred at about midday.

The First Apparition—May 13, 1917

The three seers were playing at Cova da Iria when they saw two flashes like lightning, after which they saw the Mother of God above the holm oak. She was, according to the description of Lúcia, "a Lady dressed all in white, more brilliant than the sun, shedding a light that was clearer and more intense than that of a crystal goblet filled with crystalline water and struck by the rays of the most brilliant sun." Her face, indescribably beautiful, was "neither sad nor happy, but serious," with an air of mild reproach. Her hands, joined together as if she were praying, were resting at her breast and pointing upward. A rosary hung from her right hand. Her clothes seemed to be made of light. The tunic was white. The veil, white and edged with gold, covered the head of the Virgin and descended to her feet. Neither her hair nor her ears could be seen. Lúcia could never describe her features, for it was impossible for her to fix her gaze on the dazzling heavenly face. The seers were so close to Our Lady—about a yard and a half away—that they stood within the light that radiated from and enveloped her. The conversation developed in the following manner:[1]

Our Lady: Do not be afraid; I will not harm you.

Lúcia: Where is Your Grace[2] from?

Our Lady: I am from heaven. (Our Lady raised her hand and pointed to the sky.)

Lúcia: And what does Your Grace wish of me?

Our Lady: I have come to ask you to come here for six months in succession on the thirteenth day of each month at this same hour.[3] Later

---

1. During his interview with Sister Lúcia, Walsh asked her if she had repeated the exact words in her narrations or just the general meaning of what she was told by the angel and Our Lady. Sister Lúcia answered: "The angel's words had an intense and overpowering quality, a supernatural reality that could not be forgotten. They seemed to engrave themselves exactly and indelibly upon the memory. It was different with the words of Our Lady. I could not be sure that every word was exact. It was rather the sense that came to me, and I put into words what I understood. It is not easy to explain this" (Walsh, English ed., p. 224).

Faced with the difficulty of putting what she had heard from Our Lady into words (as is common in certain mystical phenomena), Sister Lúcia always did her utmost to reproduce verbatim what the Blessed Virgin had told her. This becomes clear in Father Iongen's interrogation, part of which we reproduce below.

Father Iongen: When you revealed the secret, did you wish to limit yourself to giving the meaning of what the Blessed Virgin had told you, or did you reproduce her words verbatim?

Sister Lúcia: When I speak of the apparitions, I limit myself to the meaning of the words; when I write about them, on the contrary, I endeavor to reproduce the words verbatim. So I wanted to write the secret word for word.

Father Iongen: Are you sure you have kept everything in your memory?

Sister Lúcia: I think so.

Father Iongen: So the words of the secret were revealed in the order they were told to you. Is that it?

Sister Lúcia: Yes. (See De Marchi, pp. 308-309.)

2. Many authors use *Your Excellency*, *Madam*, and *you* instead. However, *Your Grace* seems to be a more accurate translation, as Lúcia's *Vossemecê* is the contraction of the old polite form of address *Vossa Mercê*, whose literal meaning is Your Grace.— TRANS.

3. The seers always understood that the last apparition would be in October. In fact, they were told this explicitly in the apparition of August. Therefore, the "six months in succession" begin with this apparition. The seventh, which is mentioned further on, is not part of the series.

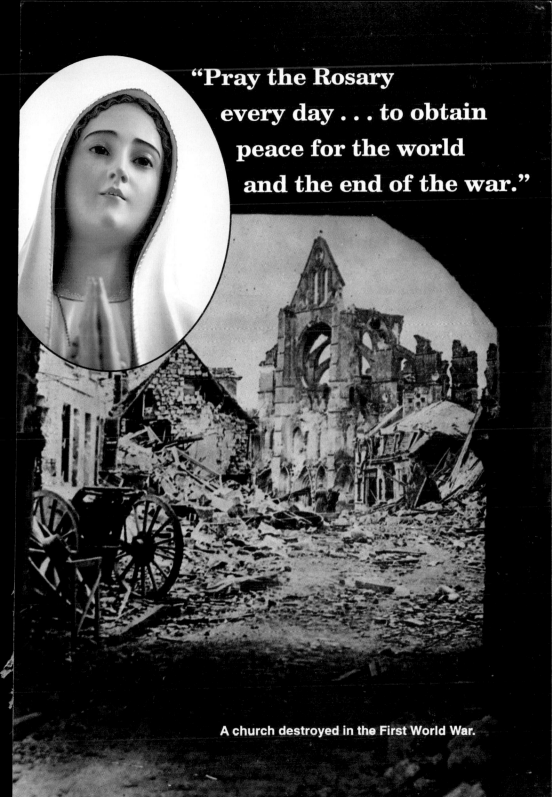

"Pray the Rosary every day . . . to obtain peace for the world and the end of the war."

A church destroyed in the First World War.

I will tell you who I am and what I want. Afterward, I will return here
a seventh time.

> *Lúcia:* And will I go to heaven, too?
> *Our Lady:* Yes, you will.
> *Lúcia:* And Jacinta?
> *Our Lady:* Also.
> *Lúcia:* And Francisco?
> *Our Lady:* Also, but he must say many Rosaries!
> *Lúcia:* Is Maria das Neves already in heaven?
> *Our Lady:* Yes, she is.
> *Lúcia:* And Amélia?
> *Our Lady:* She will be in purgatory until the end of the world.

Do you wish to offer yourselves to God to endure all the sufferings
that He may be pleased to send you, as both an act of reparation for the
sins with which He is offended and an act of supplication for the conversion of sinners?

> *Lúcia:* Yes, we do.

Our Lady: Well then, you will have much to suffer. But the grace of
God will be your comfort.

·"It was upon saying these last words, 'the grace of God...' that for
the first time she opened her hands, which emitted a most intense light
that penetrated our breasts, reaching the innermost part of our souls and
making us see ourselves in God, Who was that light, more clearly than
we can see ourselves in the best of mirrors. Then, driven by a deep
inspiration, we knelt down and repeated inwardly: 'O Most Holy Trinity, I adore Thee! My God, my God, I love Thee in the Most Blessed
Sacrament.'

"A moment later, Our Lady added, 'Pray the Rosary[4] every day to

---

4. Our Lady said "o terço," the literal translation of which is "the third," in other
words, five of the fifteen decades of the Rosary. However, the Portuguese at times also
term the fifteen decades of the Rosary *o terço*. Throughout this work, *o terço* has been
translated as the Rosary. It is interesting to note that when Our Lady appeared to Sister
Lúcia to ask for the five first Saturdays devotion she did not say "the third," but rather
"a third" (*um terço*), that is, five decades.—TRANS.

The war is going to end, but if they do not stop offending God, another even worse war will begin in the reign of Pius XI.

addresses mass meeting, n, 1938. Parisians under nan sniper fire scramble for r, 1944. Church of Our Lady air raid, Munich, 1944.

OS: THE BETTMANN ARCHIVE)

obtain peace for the world and the end of the war.'

"She immediately began to rise serenely toward the east until she disappeared far into the distance. The light that surrounded her was, so to speak, opening her way through the starry firmament." (See Memoir II, p. 126, and IV, pp. 330, 336; De Marchi, pp. 58-60; Walsh, pp. 52-53; Ayres da Fonseca, pp. 23-26; Galamba de Oliveira, pp. 63-64.)

The Second Apparition—June 13, 1917

Preceding the second apparition, the seers once again saw a great brilliance, which they called lightning, but which was really the glare of the approaching light. Some of the approximately fifty spectators who had come to the place noticed that the light of the sun became dimmer during the first few minutes of the conversation. Others said that the top of the budding holm oak bent down, as if under the weight of something, a moment before Lúcia spoke. During Our Lady's conversation with the seers, some of the bystanders heard a whispering, like the humming of a bee.

Lúcia: What does Your Grace wish of me?

Our Lady: I want you to come here on the thirteenth of next month, to pray the Rosary every day, and to learn to read.[5] I shall later say what I want. (Lúcia asked for the cure of a sick person.)

Our Lady: If he converts, he will be cured within the year.

Lúcia: I would like to ask you to take us to heaven.

Our Lady: Yes, I shall take Jacinta and Francisco soon, but you will remain here for some time yet. Jesus wishes to use you in order to make me known and loved. He wishes to establish devotion to my Immaculate Heart in the world. I promise salvation to those who embrace it; and these souls will be beloved of God like flowers arranged by me to adorn His throne.

_____

5. It was always understood that the order to learn to read was for Lúcia alone, since the other seers were soon to be taken to heaven according to the promise of Our Lady in this same apparition. However, Sister Lúcia's original Portuguese is in the plural, "*e que aprendam a ler,*" perhaps due to a slight lapse of syntax by switching from the second to the third person plural in the same sentence.

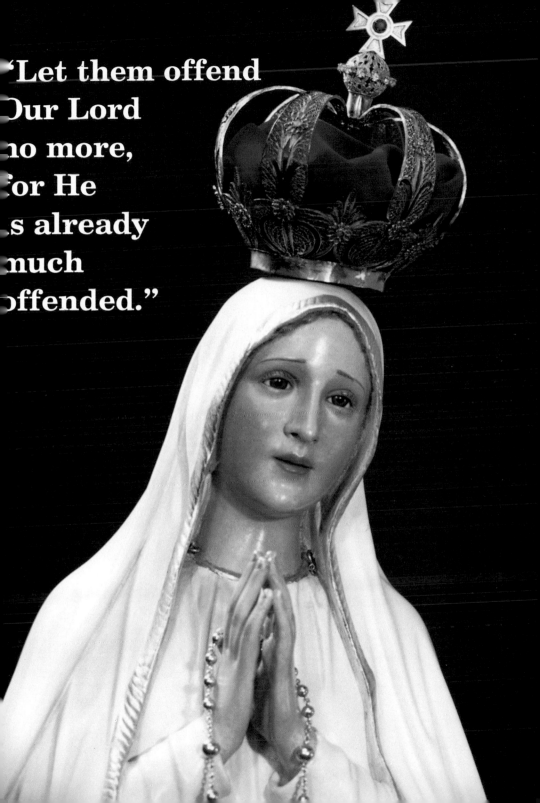

"Let them offend
Our Lord
no more,
for He
is already
much
offended."

Lúcia: Will I stay here alone?

Our Lady: No, daughter. Does that make you suffer much? Do not be dismayed. I will never forsake you. My Immaculate Heart shall be your refuge and the road that shall lead you to God.

"Upon saying these last words, she opened her hands, and for the second time she communicated to us the reflection of that intense light. We could see ourselves in it, as if immersed in God. Jacinta and Francisco seemed to be in the part of this light that went up toward heaven, and I in the part that was cast toward the ground. In front of Our Lady's right hand there was a heart encircled by thorns that seemed to pierce it. We understood that it was the Immaculate Heart of Mary, insulted by the sins of humanity and which desires reparation."[6]

When this vision ceased, the Lady, still surrounded by the light that she radiated, rose from the little tree and glided toward the east until she disappeared completely. Several persons who were closer noticed that the buds at the top of the holm oak were bent in the same direction, as if they had been drawn by the Lady's clothes. They returned to their usual position only some hours later. (See Memoir II, p. 130, and IV, pp. 334, 336; Memoirs, p. 400; De Marchi, pp. 76-78; Walsh, pp. 65-66; Ayres da Fonseca, pp. 34-36; Galamba de Oliveira, p. 70.)

The Third Apparition—July 13, 1917

Mr. Marto, father of Jacinta and Francisco, says that when the third apparition began, a little grayish cloud hovered over the holm oak, the sunlight diminished, and a cool breeze blew over the mountain range, even though it was the height of summer. He also heard something that sounded like flies inside an empty jug. The seers saw the customary glare, and immediately afterward they saw Our Lady over the holm oak.

---

6. The seers kept what they were told in the June apparition regarding the devotion to the Immaculate Heart of Mary in the strictest reserve. They even stated that Our Lady had revealed a secret to them. In her memoirs, Sister Lúcia explains that the Blessed Virgin had not requested secrecy on this point, but adds: "We felt that God moved us to do so." (See Memoir IV, p. 336.)

"If they listen to my requests, Russia will convert and there will be peace; if not, it will spread its errors throughout the world, promoting wars and persecutions of the Church."

Top: Lenin; Tanks at Red Square
Middle: Soviet missile parade.
Bottom: Cambodian genocide mass
grave; Vietnamese victims of communist aggression.

"...wars and persecutions..."

Church building next to the Berlin Wall being dynamited by communist authorities in January 1985.

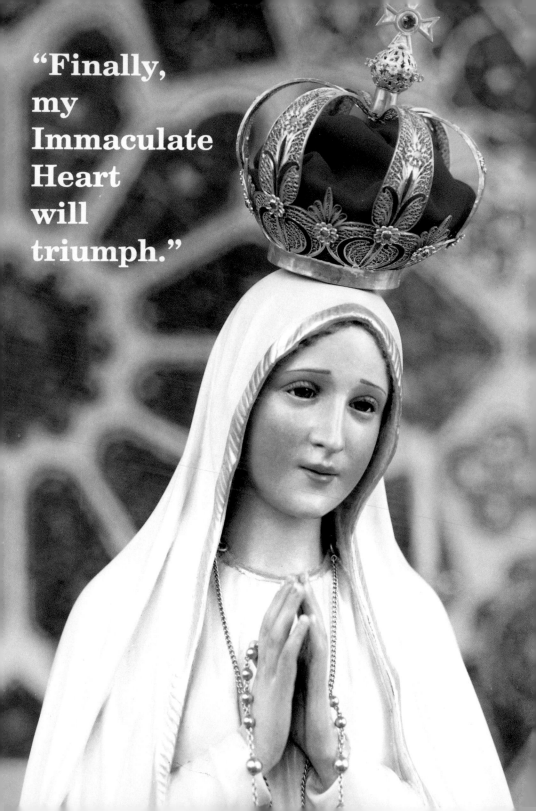

"Finally, my Immaculate Heart will triumph."

Lúcia: What does Your Grace wish of me?

Our Lady: I want you to come here on the thirteenth of next month and to continue to pray the Rosary every day in honor of Our Lady of the Rosary in order to obtain peace for the world and the end of the war, for she alone can be of any avail.

Lúcia: I would like to ask you to tell us who you are and to perform a miracle so everyone will believe that Your Grace appears to us.

Our Lady: Continue to come here every month. In October, I will tell you who I am and what I wish, and I will perform a miracle that everyone shall see so as to believe.

Lúcia then made a number of requests for conversions, cures, and other graces. Our Lady recommended the constant recitation of the Rosary; thus they would obtain those graces during the year.[7]

Then she went on: "Sacrifice yourselves for sinners and say many times, especially when you make some sacrifice, 'O Jesus, this is for love of Thee, for the conversion of sinners, and in reparation for the sins committed against the Immaculate Heart of Mary.'"

- **The First Part of the Secret:
  The Vision of Hell**

"As she said these last words," writes Sister Lúcia, "she once again opened her hands as she had done in the two previous months. The radiant light [which streamed from them] seemed to penetrate the earth,

---

7. The cited authors provide some details of the requests made by Lúcia during this apparition. One of the requests was the cure of the crippled son of Maria Carreira. Our Lady answered that she would not cure him nor relieve him of his poverty, but she said she would give him means to earn a living should he pray the Rosary every day with his family. (See De Marchi, p. 91; Ayres da Fonseca, p. 42.)

A sick woman had asked to be taken to heaven soon. Our Lady said the woman should be in no hurry, as she knew very well when to come to get her. (See De Marchi, p. 91.)

On page 86 of his book, Walsh says that Jacinta told her parents of Our Lady's wish that every family pray the Rosary daily. However, the only reference this author found to that pious practice in the accounts of the apparitions is the advice given to the son of Maria Carreira.

The three shepherd children of Fátima, Lúcia, Francisco and Jacinta.

The three seers, photographed anew shortly after the vision of hell, July 13, 1917.

and we saw, as it were, a great sea of fire; submerged in that fire were demons and souls in human shapes who resembled red-hot, black and bronze-colored embers that floated about in the blaze, borne by the flames that issued from them with clouds of smoke, falling everywhere like the showering sparks of great blazes—with neither weight nor equilibrium—amidst shrieks and groans of sorrow and despair that horrified us and made us shudder with fear.

"The devils stood out like frightful and unknown animals with horrible and disgusting shapes, but transparent like black coals that have become red-hot."

The vision lasted only a moment, during which Lúcia let out a gasp. She remarks that if it were not for Our Lady's promise to take them to heaven, the seers would have died of fright and terror.

- **The Second Part of the
  Secret: The Warning of the
  Chastisement and the Ways
  to Avoid It**

Frightened and as though pleading for help, the seers raised their eyes to Our Lady, who said with kindness and sadness:

"'You saw hell, where the souls of poor sinners go. To save them, God wishes to establish devotion to my Immaculate Heart in the world. If they do what I shall tell you, many souls will be saved and there will be peace.

"'The war is going to end, but if they do not stop offending God, another even worse war will begin in the reign of Pius XI.[8] Behold, a night illuminated by an unknown light will be the great sign that God shall give you that He is going to punish the world for its crimes by

---

8. In the declarations given in February 1946 to the Dutch Montfortist Father Iongen, Sister Lúcia confirmed having heard Our Lady say the name of Pius XI, but at the time she did not know whether Our Lady was referring to a pope or a king.

The fact that the war is understood to have begun only in the reign of Pope Pius XII presents no great difficulty for Sister Lúcia. She remarks that the annexation of Austria by Germany—and we might add various other political events at the end of the reign of Pope Pius XI—constituted the preliminary stage of the conflagration that would take shape fully some time later. (See De Marchi, p. 309.)

means of war, hunger, and persecutions of the Church and of the Holy Father.[9]

"'To prevent it [the war], I will come to ask for the consecration of Russia to my Immaculate Heart and the Communion of reparation on the first Saturdays. If they listen to my requests, Russia will convert and there will be peace; if not, it will spread its errors throughout the world, promoting wars and persecutions of the Church. The good will be martyred; the Holy Father will have much to suffer, and several nations will be annihilated.

"'Finally, my Immaculate Heart will triumph.

"'The Holy Father will consecrate Russia—which will convert—to me, and a certain period of peace will be granted to the world.

"'In Portugal, the dogma of the Faith will always be kept,' etc."

"'Do not tell anybody about this. You may tell Francisco, though.'"[10]

_____

9. Sister Lúcia regarded the extraordinary light that illuminated the skies of Europe on the night of January 25, 1938 (from 8:45 p.m. to 1:15 a.m. with brief interruptions) as "the great sign," though some astronomers considered it to be an aurora borealis. Convinced that a world war, which "would be horrible, horrible," would erupt any moment, she redoubled her efforts to obtain compliance with the requests communicated to her (see chapter IV). She wrote a letter directly to Pope Pius XI for that purpose. (See De Marchi, p. 92; Walsh, pp. 179-181; Ayres da Fonseca, p. 45.)

10. The vision of hell and the prediction of future events constitute the two known parts of the Secret of Fátima communicated to the seers in the July apparition.
Sister Lúcia points out that "the secret consists of three different parts." (See Memoir III, p. 218.) The first is the vision of hell. The second is the warning of the chastisement and how to avoid it. The third, according to Father Antonio Maria Martins, S.J. and our own conjectures, might concern the crisis in the Church, a cause of the condemnation of innumerable souls (first part of the secret) and of the chastisement that will fall upon the world (second part of the secret). In a sermon of June 29, 1972, Pope Paul VI referred to this crisis, saying that "Satan's smoke has made its way into the temple of God through some crack."

In the preface to the Brazilian edition of Sister Lúcia's writings, Father Antonio Maria Martins, S.J., categorically affirms that the third part of the secret, "the text of which has not yet been divulged, deals with the crisis in the Church." (See Memoirs, p. xviii.) The author does not explain how he came to know this, nor does he provide further clarification on the subject. At any rate, this contention is so plausible that one could almost say that the secret must deal with this very grave matter. This may explain why this part of the message has not yet been made public despite the enormous expectation that exists all over the world.

It is of interest to point out that although Memoir III ends the account of the second part of the secret with the words "and a certain period of peace will be granted to the world," in Memoir IV, Sister Lúcia concludes with, "In Portugal, the dogma of the Faith will always be kept, etc." Thus, one could infer that the dogma of the Faith will be lost in so much of the world that its preservation in Portugal is something worthy of special mention. But what does it really mean to say that the dogma of the Faith is or is not preserved in a particular country? It is difficult to say. Whatever import is attributed to this statement, Our Lady was evidently referring to a religious crisis, which increases the probability that the crisis in the Church is the theme of the third part of the secret.

Moreover, the "etc." with which Sister Lúcia concludes the narration suggests that the third part of the secret would follow at this point.

Setting these plausible conjectures aside, the examination of reality clearly shows that one of the most shocking aspects of the crisis in the Church is the leftist infiltration in Catholic milieus. This infiltration was already so alarming in 1968 that in that year, 1.6 million Brazilians, 280,000 Argentines, 105,000 Chileans, and 25,000 Uruguayans signed a petition to His Holiness Pope Paul VI requesting him to take urgent measures against it. (The memorable petition was promoted in those countries by the respective Societies for the Defense of Tradition, Family and Property. _Time_ magazine [8/23/68] reported this about the petition: "The ease with which TFP collected the signatures reflects the fact that a majority of Latinos either approve or at least tolerate [sic] Catholic conservatism.")

Now, communism is precisely the scourge with which God wishes to punish the world for its crimes: "Russia...will spread its errors throughout the world" (second part of the secret). As this idea will appear many times in this book, it is opportune to note that this can still be affirmed despite events in Russia and its empire since 1989.

While _glasnost_ and _perestroika_ and the demolishing of the Berlin Wall and the Iron Curtain were seen by many observers as signs of the softening and even the death of communism, there were then and there are now many factors that oppose such an optimistic view. Even as those policies and events were on the front pages, Russia's errors still held sway in numerous places from China to Cuba. And today we see "former" communists regaining leading positions in several countries of the former Soviet bloc as well as signs of increasing disorder there and elsewhere. Indeed, if the Soviet leviathan has disintegrated, "this disintegration has spread an even more deadly climate of crisis throughout the world," as Professor Plinio Corrêa de Oliveira writes in his masterly study _Revolution and Counter-Revolution_, (p. 131).

More importantly, these policies and events must be seen in terms of the stated goals of the communist thinkers and leaders. The communist super-state was never intended by Marx or Lenin to be the essence or final stage of communism, and Gorbachev himself affirms in his propagandistic _Perestroika: New Thinking for Our Country and the World_ (p. 34) that _perestroika_ is a refinement of communism.

Some instants later, the dialogue resumed.

Our Lady: When you pray the Rosary, after each decade say, "O my Jesus, forgive us, save us from the fire of hell; lead all souls to heaven, especially those in most need."[11]

Lúcia: Does Your Grace wish anything else of me?

Our Lady: No, today I do not wish anything else of you.

"As usual, she then began to rise toward the east until she disappeared in the expanse of the firmament."

At that point, a sound like thunder was heard, indicating that the

---

Furthermore, we must consider the way in which the errors of Russia have spread and are spreading throughout the world, not just by bloody struggles but also through socialism (which in essence is the same as communism) and a veritable cultural revolution, what Professor Corrêa de Oliveira had, in 1959, termed a revolution in the tendencies in the work just cited. The reader is referred to *Revolution and Counter-Revolution* (see bibliography) for a fuller treatment of these considerations.

All this naturally leads one to consider how much the second and third parts of the secret would conform to each other if the latter actually dealt with the crisis in the Church.

11. Slightly different versions of this prayer are in circulation. Small variations appear even in the manuscripts and interviews of Sister Lúcia. The version we quote is found in Memoir IV, pages 340 and 342, and was confirmed by the seer in an interview with Walsh. In answer to a question by Dr. Goulven, however, Sister Lúcia wrote the last phrase with this wording: "and especially help those in most need." (See Reis, *A Vidente de Fátima dialoga*, p. 39.)

This version is the most distinct one and is not mentioned outside this document. It is not known whether Father Reis transcribed it directly from the manuscript or from one of the typed copies when he included it in his work. If the latter is the case, it would be interesting to compare the manuscript with the typewritten copy of the cited matter in order to make sure no error was made during the transcription.

The seers, in saying this prayer, understood it to apply to those souls who are in the greatest danger of damnation, and not to the souls in purgatory. Sister Lúcia affirms this in a letter of May 18, 1941, to Father Gonçalves. "They adjusted it by making the last petition for the souls in purgatory because they claimed not to understand the meaning of the last words, but I believe Our Lady was referring to the souls who are in greater danger of damnation. This was the impression I had, and perhaps Your Reverence feels the same after having read what I wrote about the secret, keeping in mind that she taught us the prayers at the time of the third [apparition in] July." (See Memoirs, p. 442.) Therefore, the formula, "O my Jesus, forgive us our sins, save us from the fire of hell, have mercy on the souls in purgatory, especially the most abandoned," is certainly incorrect.

apparition had ended.[12] (See Memoir II, p. 138, and III, pp. 218, 220, and IV, pp. 336-342; De Marchi, pp. 90-93; Walsh, pp. 75-77; Ayres da Fonseca, pp. 41-46; Galamba de Oliveira, pp. 72-78; 146-147.)

The Fourth Apparition—August 15, 1917

On August 13, the day the fourth apparition was to take place, the seers could not go to Cova da Iria, as they had been abducted by the mayor of Vila Nova de Ourém, who wanted to force the secret from them. The children held fast.

---

12. Besieged after this apparition with questions about what Our Lady had told them, the seers said it was a secret.

"Good or bad?" insisted the questioners. "Good for some, bad for others," responded the children. (See De Marchi, p. 94; Walsh, English ed., p. 84.)

Before the last apparition, Canon Manuel Nunes Formigão asked Francisco and Jacinta whether the "people would be sad if they knew the secret." Their answer was "They would." (See De Marchi, pp. 151-152; Walsh, p. 121.)

Was the war of 1939-45 the punishment foretold in the apparition of July? Analysis of the prediction seems to lead to the conclusion that World War II was but the threshold of the great punishment.

Indeed, Our Lady warned that "several nations will be annihilated." To be sure, several nations were severely punished during and after the war, but it cannot be said that they were annihilated.

Moreover, once the conflagration had already ended, Sister Lúcia stated in an interview granted to Walsh on July 15, 1946 that "if this is done [the consecration of Russia], she [the Blessed Virgin] will convert Russia, and there will be peace. If this is not done, the errors of Russia will spread through every country in the world." "Does this mean, in your opinion," asked Walsh, "that every country, without exception, will be overcome by communism?" "Yes," answered the seer. (Walsh, English ed., p. 226.) (Editor's note: It is worthwhile to ponder this statement in light of the supposed demise of communism.)

Since the expansion of communism and its ideological diffusion throughout the world became more conspicuous after the war ended, it must be concluded that the punishment foretold by the Mother of God is in progress.

Finally, if the punishment had already passed, the part of the message that speaks of the victory of Mary Most Holy and the establishment of her reign, clearly indicated by the words "Finally, my Immaculate Heart will triumph," should also have been fulfilled. But the world has taken the exact opposite course.

So it seems that the terrible sufferings of World War II were just a prologue to the punishments Our Lady foretold, which are yet to be completed.

At Cova da Iria, thunder followed by lightning was heard at the usual time. The spectators noticed a small white cloud that hovered over the holm oak for a few minutes. Phenomena of coloration were observed on the faces of the people, the clothing, the trees, and the ground. Our Lady had certainly come, but she had not found the seers.

On August 15, at about four o'clock in the afternoon,[13] Lúcia was with Francisco and another cousin at Valinhos, a property belonging to one of her uncles, when the atmospheric changes that preceded the apparitions of Our Lady at Cova da Iria began to occur: a sudden cooling of the temperature and a waning of the sun. Feeling that something supernatural was approaching and enveloping them, Lúcia sent for Jacinta, who arrived in time to see Our Lady appear—heralded as before by a bright light—over a holm oak slightly larger than the one at Cova da Iria.

Lúcia: What does Your Grace wish of me?
Our Lady: I want you to continue to go to Cova da Iria on the thir-

_____

13. There exists some doubt regarding this date. Sister Lúcia herself does not remember it precisely. In Memoirs II and IV she says that it was on this day. But in a letter to Dr. Goulven, she opts for the 19th, adding on the margin: "I am more inclined to this date, because if it had been on the 15th, we would have spent only one full day in prison, and I remember that we were there longer." (See Reis, *A Vidente de Fátima dialoga*, p. 43.)

During the canonical investigation of July 8, 1924, Lúcia gave a detailed, day-by-day account of her imprisonment with the other seers and said that the three returned from Vila Nova de Ourém on the 16th. Thus, most authors record August 19 as the correct date, which would be the following Sunday, since the seer remembers that the apparition took place on a holy day of obligation.

But in Memoirs II and IV, as well as in the canonical investigation, Sister Lúcia affirms decisively that the apparition of Valinhos occurred on the same day she returned from Vila Nova de Ourém. If the apparition had actually occurred on the 19th, this would mean that the children were imprisoned for six days, since they were taken away on the 13th. But, again, this seems excessive.

Galamba de Oliveira (on page 83 of his book) decided on the 15th, explaining that Lúcia might have missed the count by one day and night when she testified before the canonical commission in 1924.

**Francisco, Lúcia and Jacinta pose with pilgrims at
the site of the apparitions at Cova da Iria.**

**Erection of the Chapel of the Apparitions at Cova da Iria was
begun on August 6, 1918. Blown up on March 6, 1922 by
enemies of religion, the chapel was restored soon after.**

teenth of each month and to continue to pray the Rosary every day. On the last month, I will perform the miracle for all to believe.[14]

Lúcia: What does Your Grace want done with the money that the people leave at Cova da Iria?

Our Lady: Have two portable stands made. You and Jacinta with two other girls dressed in white carry one of them, and let Francisco carry the other one with three other boys. The portable stands are for the feast of Our Lady of the Rosary. The money that is left over should be contributed to the chapel that they shall build.[15]

Lúcia: I would like to ask you for the healing of some sick persons.

Our Lady: Yes, I will cure some during the year.

"Becoming sadder, she recommended anew the practice of mortification, saying lastly, 'Pray, pray much, and make sacrifice for sinners, for many souls go to hell because there is no one to sacrifice and pray for them.'

"As usual, she then began to rise toward the east."

The seers cut boughs off the tree over which Our Lady had appeared to them and took them home. The boughs gave off a uniquely sweet fragrance. (See Memoir II, p. 150, and IV, pp. 342, 344; De Marchi, pp. 127-129; Walsh, pp. 109-110; Ayres da Fonseca, pp. 61-62; Galamba de Oliveira, p. 89.)

The Fifth Apparition—September 13, 1917

A crowd estimated at twenty thousand observed atmospheric phenomena similar to those of the previous apparitions: the sudden cooling of the air, a dimming of the sun to the point where the stars could be seen, and a rain resembling iridescent petals or snowflakes that disap-

_____

14. At this point, De Marchi adds these words of Our Lady: "If they had not taken you to the town [meaning Vila Nova de Ourém], the miracle would be even greater." No other author includes this sentence, and it does not appear in the memoirs of Sister Lúcia.

15. According to Lúcia's declarations to the pastor of the parish of Fátima on August 21, 1917, which are confirmed by her replies in the canonical investigation of July 8, 1924, the reference to the chapel belongs in the fifth apparition. That is where De Marchi includes it. (See De Marchi, p. 127.)

peared before touching the ground. This time, a luminous globe was noticed which moved slowly and majestically through the sky from east to west and, at the end of the apparition, in the opposite direction. The seers saw a light, and, immediately following this, they saw Our Lady over the holm oak.

Our Lady: Continue to pray the Rosary to obtain the end of the war. In October, Our Lord will also come, as well as Our Lady of Sorrows and Our Lady of Mount Carmel, and Saint Joseph with the Child Jesus, to bless the world. God is pleased with your sacrifices, but He does not want you to sleep with the ropes; wear them only during the day.[16]

Lúcia: They have requested me to ask you for many things, for the cure of some sick persons, of a deaf-mute.

Our Lady: Yes, I will cure some, others not.[17] In October, I will perform a miracle for all to believe.

"And rising, she disappeared in the same manner as before." (See Memoir II, p. 156, and IV, pp. 346, 348; De Marchi, pp. 138-139; Walsh, pp. 115-116; Ayres da Fonseca, pp. 70-71; Galamba de Oliveira, p. 93.)

The Sixth and Last Apparition—October 13, 1917

As on the other occasions, the seers first saw a bright light, and then they saw Our Lady over the holm oak.

Lúcia: What does Your Grace wish of me?

Our Lady: I wish to tell you that I want a chapel built here in my honor. I am the Lady of the Rosary. Continue to pray the Rosary every

---

16. The children had started to wear a thick rough cord around their waists for penance. They did not remove it even at bedtime, which often prevented them from sleeping the whole night. This explains Our Lady's praise and suggestion.

17. At this point, De Marchi adds, "Our Lord does not trust them all." In the replies to Dr. Goulven, Sister Lúcia says that she does not remember having said this. (See Reis, *A Vidente de Fátima dialoga*, p. 45.)

De Marchi also includes the following request of *Lúcia:* "So many believe that I am [such] an impostor and a cheat that they say I deserve to be hanged and burned. Will you please perform a miracle so that all of them can believe?"

None of this appears in the memoirs of Sister Lúcia.

day. The war is going to end, and the soldiers will soon return to their homes.

Lúcia: I have many things to ask you: if you would cure some sick persons, and if you would convert some sinners....

Our Lady: Some yes, others no.[18] They must amend their lives and ask forgiveness for their sins.

"Becoming sadder, she added, 'Let them offend Our Lord no more, for He is already much offended.'

Then, opening her hands, Our Lady shone the light issuing from them onto the sun, and as she rose, her own radiance continued to be cast onto the sun."

At that moment, Lúcia cried, "Look at the sun!"

Once Our Lady had disappeared in the expanse of the firmament, three scenes followed in succession, symbolizing first the joyful mysteries of the Rosary, then the sorrowful mysteries, and, finally, the glorious mysteries. Lúcia alone saw the three scenes; Francisco and Jacinta saw only the first.

The first scene: Saint Joseph appeared beside the sun with the Child Jesus and Our Lady of the Rosary. It was the Holy Family. The Virgin was dressed in white with a blue mantle. Saint Joseph was also dressed in white, and the Child Jesus in light red. Saint Joseph blessed the crowd, making the Sign of the Cross three times. The Child Jesus did the same.

The second scene: This was followed by the vision of Our Lady of Sorrows, without the sword in her breast, and of Our Lord overwhelmed with sorrow on the way to Calvary. Our Lord made the Sign of the Cross to bless the people.

Lúcia could only see the upper part of Our Lord's body.

The third scene: Finally, Our Lady of Mount Carmel, crowned queen of heaven and earth, appeared in a glorious vision with the Child Jesus in her bosom.

While these scenes took place, the great throng of about seventy

---

18. In a letter of May 18, 1941 to Father José Bernardo Gonçalves, S.J., Sister Lúcia clarifies this point by explaining that Our Lady said she would grant some of these graces within the year, and others not. (See Memoirs, p. 442.)

thousand spectators witnessed the miracle of the sun.

It had rained all during the apparition. At the end of the conversation between Our Lady and Lúcia—when the Blessed Virgin rose and Lúcia shouted, "Look at the sun!"—the clouds opened up, revealing the sun as an immense silver disk. It shone with an intensity never before seen, but was not blinding. This lasted only an instant. Then the immense ball began to "dance." The sun began to spin rapidly like a gigantic circle of fire. Then it stopped momentarily, only to begin spinning vertiginously again. Its rim became scarlet; whirling, it scattered red flames across the sky. Their light was reflected on the ground, on the trees, on the bushes, and on the very faces and clothing of the people, which took on brilliant hues and changing colors.

After performing this bizarre pattern three times, the globe of fire seemed to tremble, shake, and then plunge in a zigzag toward the terrified crowd.

All this lasted about ten minutes. Finally, the sun zigzagged back to its original place and once again became still and brilliant, shining with its everyday brightness.

The cycle of the apparitions had ended.

Many people noticed that their clothes, soaking wet from the rain, had suddenly dried.

The miracle of the sun was also seen by numerous witnesses up to twenty-five miles away from the place of the apparition. (See Memoir II, p. 162, and IV, pp. 348, 350; De Marchi, pp. 165-166; Walsh, pp. 129-131; Ayres da Fonseca, pp. 91-93; Galamba de Oliveira, pp. 95-97.)

Lúcia and Jacinta

Chapter III

Some Private Visions

In the short time they spent on earth after the apparitions, and even during the time of the apparitions, Francisco and Jacinta had several private visions. We will relate here the principal ones, which are those of Jacinta.

"I Saw the Holy Father..."

On one occasion, at about midday, near the well of the house of Lúcia's parents, Jacinta asked Lúcia, "Did you not see the Holy Father?"

"No."

"I cannot say how, but I saw the Holy Father in a very large house, kneeling beside a table with his hands on his face. He was crying. Many people were outside the house. Some were throwing stones at him; others were cursing him and saying foul words to him. Poor Holy Father, we have to pray much for him!" (See Memoir III, p. 228; De Marchi, pp. 98-99; Walsh, p. 85; Ayres da Fonseca, p. 136.)

On an afternoon in August 1917, while the seers were sitting on the boulders of the knoll of Cabeço, Jacinta suddenly began to say the prayer the angel had taught them and, after a deep silence, said to her cousin: "Do you not see so many thoroughfares, roads, and fields full of people weeping with hunger and having nothing to eat? And the Holy Father praying in a church before the Immaculate Heart of Mary? And many people praying with him?" (See Memoir III, p. 228; De Marchi, p. 99; Walsh, p. 84; Ayres da Fonseca, p. 137.)

Lúcia, in Jacinta's home one day, found her very pensive and asked her, "Jacinta, what are you thinking about?"

"About the war that is to come. So many will die! And almost all of them will go to hell! Many homes will be razed, and many priests will be killed. Listen, I am going to heaven, and when one night you see the light the Lady told us would appear before all this, you flee to heaven also." (See Memoir III, p. 228; De Marchi, p. 238; Walsh, p. 85; Ayres da Fonseca, pp. 161-162.)

The Last Visions of Jacinta

At the end of October 1918, Francisco and Jacinta fell ill, almost at the same time. When Lúcia visited them, she found Jacinta elated. The latter explained:

"Our Lady came to see us and said that she is coming to take Francisco to heaven very soon. She asked me if I still wanted to convert more sinners. I told her I did. She told me I would be taken to a hospital and that I would suffer greatly there, but that I should suffer for the conversion of sinners, in reparation for the sins committed against the Immaculate Heart of Mary, and for the love of Jesus. I asked if you would be going with me. She said you would not. This is what hurts me most. She said my mother would take me, and after that I will remain there alone!" (See Memoir I, p. 70; De Marchi, p. 227; Walsh, p. 146; Ayres da Fonseca, p. 153.)

Lúcia frequently visited the seers during their illness. They would converse at length about the events in which they had been protagonists. We transcribe here some of Jacinta's observations:

"It will not be long before I go to heaven. You will stay here to make known God's wish to establish devotion to the Immaculate Heart of Mary in the world. When the time comes for you to speak, do not hide. Tell everybody that God grants us His graces through the Immaculate Heart of Mary, that they should ask her for them, that the Heart of Jesus wants the Immaculate Heart of Mary to be honored along with His, that they should ask the Immaculate Heart of Mary for peace because God has placed it in her keeping. Oh, if I could only put into everybody's heart the flame that burns in my breast, making me love the Hearts of Jesus and Mary so much!" (See Memoir III, p. 234; De Marchi, p. 244; Walsh, p. 156.)

"You know, Our Lord is very sad because Our Lady told us He should not be offended anymore since He was already much offended, but

"Do you not see so many thoroughfares, roads, and fields full of people weeping with hunger and having nothing to eat?"

Starving refugees in Ethiopia

AP WIDE WORLD

nobody paid attention. People continue to commit the same sins." (See Memoir III, p. 236; De Marchi, p. 243; Walsh, p. 157.)

At the end of December 1919, Our Lady again appeared to Jacinta, who thus related the event to her cousin:

"She told me I am going to another hospital in Lisbon,[1] and that I will not see you or my parents again. After having suffered much, I will die alone, but I should not be afraid because she will be there to take me to heaven." (See Memoir I, pp. 74, 76; De Marchi, p. 245; Walsh, p. 157; Ayres da Fonseca, p. 162.)

"Who Taught You All These Things?"

Taken to Lisbon, Jacinta first stayed in an orphanage adjoining the Church of Our Lady of Miracles and was later taken to the Dona Estefânia Hospital. In the orphanage, she was attended by Mother Maria da Purificação Godinho, who wrote down—though not always verbatim—her last words.

Some of them, imbued with a prophetic tone and full of unction and teachings, are reproduced below. Father De Marchi published them grouped by subject matter.

• On War

"Our Lady said that there is much war and dissension in the world."

"Wars are nothing but punishments for the sins of the world."

"Our Lady can no longer hold back the arm of her beloved Son from the world. It is necessary to do penance. If people change their ways, Our Lord will still spare the world; but if they do not, the chastisement will come."

"Our Lord is profoundly indignant at the sins and crimes committed in Portugal. For this reason, a terrible social cataclysm threatens our country, particularly the city of Lisbon. It seems that a civil war of anarchic or communist character will break out, accompanied by sackings, assassinations, fires, and devastations of all kinds. The capital will be changed into a veritable image of hell. When Divine Justice, out-

---

1. In July 1919, Jacinta had been taken to the hospital of Vila Nova de Ourém, where she had remained for two months.

raged, inflicts so frightful a punishment, all who can should flee from this city. This punishment now predicted should be announced gradually and with due discretion." (See De Marchi, p. 255; Walsh, pp. 160-161.)

"If men do not change their ways, Our Lady will send the world a punishment the like of which has never been seen. It will fall first...upon Spain." (See De Marchi, p. 92.)

Jacinta also spoke of "great world events that would take place around 1940." (See De Marchi, p. 92.)

• On Priests and Rulers

"My godmother, pray much for sinners! Pray much for priests! Pray much for religious! Priests should only occupy themselves with the affairs of the Church. Priests should be pure, very pure. The disobedience of priests and religious to their superiors and to the Holy Father greatly offends Our Lord.

"My godmother, pray much for those who govern! Woe to those who persecute the religion of Our Lord! If the government left the Church in peace and gave freedom to the holy Faith, it would be blessed by God."[2] (See De Marchi, pp. 255-256; Walsh p. 161.)

• On Sin

"The sins that lead more souls to hell are the sins of the flesh."

"Fashions that will greatly offend Our Lord will appear. People who serve God should not follow fashions. The Church has no fashions. Our Lord is always the same."

"The sins of the world are very great."

"If men knew what eternity is, they would do everything to change their lives."

"Men are lost because they do not think of the death of Our Lord and do not do penance."

---

2. The reader must bear in mind that with the anti-clerical revolution of 1910, the separation of Church and state was decreed, Church property was confiscated, religious congregations were dissolved, and the use of religious garb was forbidden. It was also stipulated that "ministers of religion enjoy no privileges."—Trans.

"Many marriages are not good; they do not please Our Lord, and they are not of God."

- **On Christian Virtue**

"My godmother, do not walk in the midst of luxury. Flee from riches. Be very fond of holy poverty and silence."

"Have much charity even for those who are bad. Speak ill of no one and flee from those who do so. Be very patient, for patience leads us to heaven. Mortification and sacrifices greatly please Our Lord."

"Confession is a sacrament of mercy. Therefore, one must approach the confessional with confidence and joy. Without confession there is no salvation."

"The Mother of God wants more virgin souls who bind themselves to her by the vow of chastity."

"To be a woman religious, it is necessary to be very pure in soul and body."

"Do you know what it means to be pure?" asked Mother Godinho.

"I do. I do. To be pure in body is to keep chastity. To be pure in soul is not to commit sins, not to look at what one should not see, not to steal, never to lie, always to tell the truth however hard it may be."

"Those who do not keep the promises they make to Our Lady will never succeed in their affairs."

"Doctors do not have light to cure the sick properly because they do not have love of God."

"Who taught you all these things?" asked Mother Godinho.

"It was Our Lady, but some I think of myself. I very much like to think." (See De Marchi, pp. 254-256; Walsh, pp. 161-162.)

Noticing that many visitors chatted and laughed in the chapel of the orphanage, Jacinta asked Mother Godinho to warn them of the lack of respect for the Real Presence this represented. When this measure did not bring about satisfactory results, she asked that the cardinal be advised that "Our Lady does not want people to talk in church." (See De Marchi, p. 252; Walsh, p. 160.)

Jacinta's Last Days

During her short stay in the hospital, Jacinta was favored with new visits of Our Lady, who told her the day and hour she would die. Four days before taking her to heaven, the Blessed Virgin took away all her pain.

On the days prior to her death, someone asked her if she wanted to see her mother. Jacinta answered: "My family will remain a short time on earth and soon will meet in heaven.... Our Lady will appear again, but not to me, because I will surely die as she told me." (See De Marchi, p. 262.)

On February 20, 1920, Our Lady came to take Jacinta. She was buried in the cemetery of Vila Nova de Ourém. Francisco had given up his soul to God on April 4 of the previous year and been buried in the cemetery of Fátima.

On September 12, 1935, Jacinta's mortal remains were transferred to the cemetery of Fátima, where they were deposited in a tomb built especially for her and her brother. The tombstone bore a simple epitaph: "Here lie the mortal remains of Francisco and Jacinta, to whom Our Lady appeared."

Later (in 1951 and 1952, respectively), their precious remains were taken to the crypt of the Basilica of Fátima, where they remain to this day.

The preparatory canonical processes for the beatification of the two seers of Fátima were officially begun in 1949. Information regarding graces obtained through the intercession of the Servants of God Francisco and Jacinta should be directed to the vice-postulator of the cause at Paço Episcopal, Leiria, Portugal.

Lúcia

Chapter IV

Sister Lúcia's Mission

A s we said before, at the time of the second apparition, when Lúcia asked to be taken to heaven together with her cousins, Our Lady answered: "Yes, I shall take Jacinta and Francisco soon, but you will remain here for some time yet. Jesus wishes to use you in order to make me known and loved. He wishes to establish devotion to my Immaculate Heart in the world."

These words clearly indicate that Lúcia, aside from being the trustee of the secrets revealed by Our Lady, would remain on this earth to carry out a specific mission.

We should recall that during the first apparition, on May 13, Our Lady announced: "I have come to ask you to come here for six months in succession on the thirteenth of each month at this same hour. Later I will tell you who I am and what I want. Afterward, I will return here a seventh time."

Therefore, a seventh apparition of Our Lady would take place at Cova da Iria. When? What might Our Lady wish to communicate or show to mankind?

Whatever it may be, it seems reasonable to believe that it will once again fall upon Sister Lúcia to be the confidante of Our Lady at Cova da Iria.

Consequently, this is one of the great expectations of the Fátima story, unless this seventh apparition has already occurred secretly.

Lúcia's Itinerary

On June 17, 1921, Lúcia left Aljustrel and was admitted as a boarding pupil in the school of the Sisters of Saint Dorothy at Vilar, a suburb of Porto. On October 24, 1925, she entered the Institute of the Sisters of

Saint Dorothy and was accepted as a postulant in that congregation's convent of Tuy, just across the Spanish border.

On October 2, 1926, Lúcia became a novice. On October 3, 1928, she took her first vows as a lay sister. Six years later, on the same day in October, she took her perpetual vows. She took the religious name of Sister Maria of Sorrows.

During the communist revolution in Spain, she was transferred for safety reasons to the school of Sardão at Vila Nova de Gaia, where she remained for some time.

On May 20, 1946, Sister Lúcia was again able to see the sites of the apparitions on a visit to Cova da Iria, Loca do Cabeço, and the property of Valinhos.

On March 25, 1948, she left the Institute of the Sisters of Saint Dorothy to enter the Carmel of Saint Joseph in Coimbra; she took the name of Sister Maria Lúcia of the Immaculate Heart,[1] taking the habit of Saint Teresa on May 13 of the same year. On May 31, 1949, she was professed as a Discalced Carmelite.

The Revelations Subsequent to 1917

In the secret given in July, Our Lady had said, "I will come to ask for the consecration of Russia to my Immaculate Heart and the Communion of reparation on the first Saturdays."

In other words, the message of Fátima was not definitively concluded with the cycle of apparitions at Cova da Iria in 1917.

---

1. Some authors say "Sister Maria of the Immaculate Heart."
In a letter to Sister Lúcia's former spiritual director, Father José Aparício, dated May 27, 1948, the bishop of Coimbra refers to the reasons why she left the Institute of the Sisters of Saint Dorothy to enter the Carmel of that city. "The seer did indeed move to the Carmel of this city on March 25 because the Holy Father, at her request, ordered me not to put any obstacles to her being transferred in view of the fact that she was often disturbed by many visitors, some of whom were quite obnoxious and curious, and tormented her to no one's avail.... She says she never felt so much peace and happiness as in that shelter. She would not exchange it for anything in the world. Because of the Holy Father's wish, she receives no letters or visitors, but I write to her about the needs of people who recommend themselves to her. To date, there have been no exceptions....Only those who obtain permission from the Holy See can visit her." (See Mariz, p. 32.)

• The Five First Saturdays
   Devotion

On December 10, 1925, the Blessed Virgin, with the Child Jesus at her side above a luminous cloud, appeared to Lúcia in her cell at the Dorothean house of Pontevedra. Placing one of her hands on Lúcia's shoulder, she showed her a heart surrounded by thorns that she had in her other hand. The Child Jesus, pointing to it, entreated the seer with the following words: "Have pity on the Heart of your Blessed Mother, which is pierced and covered with thorns by ungrateful men at every moment with no one to make an act of reparation to remove them."

The Blessed Virgin added: "My daughter, look at my Heart surrounded with the thorns with which ungrateful men pierce me constantly through blasphemies and ingratitude. You, at least, try to console me, and tell men that I promise to assist at the hour of death with the graces necessary for salvation all those who, on the first Saturdays of five consecutive months, confess, receive Holy Communion, pray a Rosary (see footnote 4, Chp. II), and keep me company for a quarter of an hour meditating on the fifteen mysteries with the intention of offering me reparation." (See Memoirs, p. 400; Ayres da Fonseca, pp. 350-351; Walsh, pp. 196; De Marchi, English ed., pp. 152-153; Fazenda, p. x-xi.)

On February 15, 1926, the Child Jesus again appeared to Lúcia in Pontevedra, asking her if she had yet divulged this devotion to His Blessed Mother. The seer explained the difficulties presented by her confessor, adding that the mother superior was ready to divulge it, but that the confessor had said that the mother superior alone could not succeed. Jesus answered, "It is true that your superior alone can do nothing, but with My grace she can do everything."

Lúcia presented the problem that going to confession on Saturdays posed for some people and requested that a confession within a period of eight days before and eight days after the first Saturday be valid. Jesus answered, "Yes, it can even be within many more days, provided they are in the state of grace when they receive Me and have the intention of offering reparation to the Immaculate Heart of Mary."

Sister Lúcia further raised the possibility that some people might forget to make that intention when they confessed. Our Lord answered, "They can make it in the following confession, using the first opportunity they have to confess." (See Memoirs, P. 400; Fazenda, pp. xi-xii; Ayres da Fonseca, p. 351; De Marchi, English ed., p. 153.)

During the vigil that Sister Lúcia kept on the eve of May 30, 1930, Our Lord spoke in her interior and solved yet another difficulty. "The practice of this devotion will be equally acceptable on the Sunday following the First Saturday, whenever My priests, for just reasons, so grant it to souls." (See Memoirs, p. 410.)

• **Revealing The Secret**

On December 17, 1927, Sister Lúcia approached the tabernacle in the chapel of the Dorothean house of Tuy to ask Our Lord how she was to carry out her confessor's order to write about some graces she had received from God, since the secret confided to her by the Blessed Virgin was connected with them. With a clear voice, Jesus made her hear the following words: "My daughter, write what they ask you, as well as everything that the Blessed Virgin revealed to you in the apparition in which she spoke about this devotion [to the Immaculate Heart of Mary]. As for the rest of the secret, remain silent." (See Memoirs, p. 400; Ayres da Fonseca, p. 34.)

In compliance with this order, Sister Lúcia made public what had happened during the apparition of June.

In 1941, when the bishop of Leiria ordered the seer to recall everything of interest in Jacinta's life for a new book that was going to be published, she revealed two of the three parts of the July secret after obtaining permission from heaven.

She wrote: "The secret is composed of three different parts, two of which I am going to reveal.

"Well, then the first was the vision of hell."

She continues with the narration of the two parts of the secret as they appear in the description of the July apparition. (See Memoir III, pp. 216-220; Ayres da Fonseca, pp. 43-44; Galamba de Oliveira, p. 146.)

The seer wrote the last part of the secret (see footnote 10, Chp. II) between January 2 and January 9, 1944, in a letter addressed to the Most Reverend José Alves Correia da Silva, bishop of Leiria, through the titular bishop of Gurza, the Most Reverend Manuel Maria Ferreira da Silva, her old confessor in Porto. According to declarations of Sister Lúcia, this document was not to be made public before 1960.[2] It was taken by the Most Reverend João Pereira Venâncio, auxiliary bishop of Leiria, to the apostolic nuncio in Lisbon. The nuncio (later Fernando Cardinal Cento) took it to the Vatican, which it entered on April 16, 1957. It is not known whether Pius XII came to know it. It was, however, read by Pope John XXIII and by Alfredo Cardinal Ottaviani, Prefect of the Sacred Congregation of the Holy Office (now Congregation for the Doctrine of the Faith). Immediately thereafter, the document was sent to the secret archives of the Vatican. (See Reis, *Síntese crítica*, p. 69; *A Vidente de Fátima dialoga*, p. 70.)

A reliable source has revealed that Sister Lúcia wrote this part of the secret at the urging of the bishop of Leiria during a grave illness she had in 1939. (See Walsh, pp. 185-186.)

Details of another apparition of Our Lord to Sister Lúcia, also in 1927, are not known. (See Walsh, p. 195.)

- **The Consecration of Russia
  to the Immaculate Heart of
  Mary**

On June 13, 1929, Sister Lúcia had a sublime vision of the Holy Trinity and the Immaculate Heart of Mary, in which the consecration of Russia was requested.

"I had asked," Sister Lúcia wrote, "and obtained permission from my superiors and my confessor to make the Holy Hour on Thursdays from eleven o'clock until midnight. Being alone one night, I knelt between the balustrades in the middle of the chapel and prostrated myself to say the prayers of the angel. I grew tired, so I rose to a kneeling position and continued saying the prayers with my arms outstretched in the form of a cross.

"The only light was that of the sanctuary lamp. Suddenly, the whole chapel was illuminated with a supernatural light, and a cross of light that reached to the ceiling appeared over the altar. A man [the Eternal Father] could be seen from the waist up in the midst of a brighter light

---

2. According to her interview with Father Iongen. (See Reis, *A Vidente de Fátima dialoga*, p. 82.)

on the upper part of the cross. He had a dove of light [the Holy Ghost] at his chest. The body of another man [Our Lord Jesus Christ] was nailed to the cross. Suspended in the air just below His waist was a chalice and a large host on which fell some drops of blood from the face and the wound in the side of the Crucified. These drops ran down the host into the chalice. Our Lady was under the right arm of the cross [it was Our Lady of Fátima, who held her Immaculate Heart in her left hand, without a sword or roses, but with a crown of thorns and flames]. Under the left arm, large letters that seemed to be made of crystal-clear water running onto the altar formed these words: 'Grace and Mercy.'

"I understood I was being shown the mystery of the Most Holy Trinity, and I received lights about this mystery that I am not permitted to reveal.

"Then Our Lady said to me: 'The moment has arrived wherein God is asking the Holy Father to consecrate Russia to my Immaculate Heart in union with all the bishops of the world. He promises to save it by this means. The souls whom the justice of God condemns for sins committed against me are so many that I have come to ask for reparation. Do penance for this intention and pray.'"[3] (See Memoirs, pp. 462, 464.)

Through her confessors and the bishop of Leiria, the seer sent this request of Our Lady to Pope Pius XI that same year. The pontiff promised to take it into consideration. (See De Marchi, p. 311; Walsh, p. 198.)

In a letter to her confessor, Father José Bernardo Gonçalves, S.J., dated May 29, 1930, Sister Lúcia explained that Our Lord made her feel His divine presence in the depth of her heart and urged her to ask the Holy Father for the approval of the reparative devotion of the first Saturdays. These are the words of the seer: "If I am not mistaken, the good Lord promises to put an end to the persecution in Russia if the Holy Father deigns to make a solemn and public act of reparation and consecration of Russia to the Sacred Hearts of Jesus and Mary and orders all the bishops of the Catholic world to do the same. The Holy Father must also promise to approve and recommend the reparative

_____

3. Transcription by Father José Bernardo Gonçalves, S.J., of a manuscript of Sister Lúcia, which apparently no longer exists. (See Memoirs, Brazilian and Portuguese eds., p. 193.)

devotion already indicated in return for the ceasing of this persecution."
(See Memoirs, p. 404.)

Later, through another interior communication, Our Lord complained to Sister Lúcia that the consecration of Russia had not been made. "They did not want to heed My request. They will repent like the king of France and will make it, but it will be too late.[4] Russia will already have spread its errors throughout the world, promoting wars and persecutions of the Church. The Holy Father will have much to suffer." (See Memoirs, p. 464.)

On January 21, 1935, in another letter to Father José Bernardo Gonçalves, S.J., Sister Lúcia stated that "Our Lord was quite displeased because His request had not been carried out." (See Memoirs, p. 412.)

Writing to the same priest on May 18, 1936, Sister Lúcia explained: "About the other question—as to whether or not it would be appropriate to insist in order to obtain the consecration of Russia—my reply is almost the same as my previous ones: I regret it has not been done yet, but the same God who requested it is the one who has so permitted this.... Whether it is appropriate to insist or not, I do not know. It seems to me that if the Holy Father did it right now, God would accept it and would fulfill His promise, and, in so doing, the Holy Father would no doubt gladden Our Lord and the Immaculate Heart of Mary.

I have spoken to Our Lord inwardly about the subject, and not too long ago I asked Him why He would not convert Russia without the Holy Father making that consecration.

_____

4. This is an allusion to the promise Our Lord made to Louis XIV through Saint Margaret Mary Alacoque. Our Lord promised to give the king a life of grace and eternal glory, as well as victory over his enemies, if he would consecrate himself to the Sacred Heart, let It reign in his palace, paint It on his banners, and have It engraved on his coat of arms.

As of 1792, after Louis XVI had been imprisoned in the Tower of the Temple, this request had still not been heeded. This king then made the vow to consecrate himself, his family, and his kingdom to the Sacred Heart of Jesus if he regained his freedom, the crown, and royal power. It was too late; the king left prison only for his execution.

**The Most Reverend José Alves Correia da Silva, bishop of Leiria,
with an envelope containing the secret delivered to him at the
Fonseca Hospital in Valencia do Minho, 1940.**

"'Because I want My whole Church to acknowledge that consecration as a triumph of the Immaculate Heart of Mary, so as to subsequently extend the devotion to it and place it alongside the devotion to My Sacred Heart.'

"'But, my God, the Holy Father will not believe me unless You move him with a special inspiration.'

"'The Holy Father! Pray very much for the Holy Father! He will do it, but it will be late. Nevertheless, the Immaculate Heart of Mary will save Russia, which has been entrusted to it.'" (See Memoirs, pp. 412, 414.)

Again writing to Father Gonçalves, on April 24, 1940, she says: "If He wanted to, He could hasten that cause. But He will let it go slowly to punish the world. His justice, provoked by our sins, demands it thus. Sometimes He becomes annoyed not only at grave sins, but also at our laxity and negligence in heeding His requests.... Sins are many, but, above all, the negligence of souls whom He expected to serve Him with ardor is much greater today. The number of souls who are with Him is very small."[5] (See Memoirs, pp. 420, 422.)

Sister Lúcia returned to the same thoughts in a letter—also to Father Gonçalves—on August 18, 1940, writing:

"I suppose it pleases Our Lord that there is someone who is concerned about His vicar on earth fulfilling His wishes. But the Holy Father will not comply with them now. He doubts they are real, and explicably so. Our good Lord could show clearly through some prodigy that it is He who is asking, but He takes this opportunity to punish the world with His justice for so many crimes and to prepare it for a more

---

5. As can be seen, Sister Lúcia follows closely what goes on in the world in connection with the requests of Our Lord and Our Lady. But her knowledge of the facts is not always acquired through normal channels of information. In a letter to Father Gonçalves on January 21, 1940, she writes: "I read things of this nature [some magazine articles they wanted her to see] only when my superiors explicitly order me to do so.... As for the rest, my superiors want me to remain ignorant of what is going on, and I am content with that. I have no curiosity. When Our Lord wishes me to know something, He takes it upon Himself to let me know. He has so many means at His disposal for this." (See Memoirs, p. 420.)

complete return to Him.[6] The proof that He gives us is the special protection the Immaculate Heart of Mary affords Portugal in view of the consecration made to it.[7]

"The people you tell me about have good reason to be frightened. All that would also happen to us had our prelates not heeded the requests of our good Lord nor so earnestly implored His mercy and the protection of the Immaculate Heart of our good heavenly Mother. But in our country there are still many crimes and sins, and, since now is the hour of God's justice upon the world, it is necessary to continue praying. For

---

6. In the second part of the secret, Our Lady foretold the triumph of her Immaculate Heart, which will take place after the chastisement by which God shall punish the world for its crimes. In this document, Sister Lúcia refers to "a more complete return" of the world to God. All this fits in admirably with the reign of Mary prophesied by Saint Louis-Marie Grignion de Montfort in his renowned *Treatise on the True Devotion to the Blessed Virgin* and in his "Fiery Prayer" asking for the apostles of the last times. According to the saint, Our Lady will occupy a central role in the life of both the religious and the temporal societies in the reign of Mary, exercising a special dominion over souls. A splendid reflowering of Holy Church and Christian civilization will thus take place. The message of Fátima is a magnificent promise of the fulfillment of this prophetic vision in our days.

7. In May of 1936 the Portuguese bishops gathered at Fátima and vowed to return there in a plenary assembly if their country remained free from the Red danger so fearsomely close. (The communist revolution in Spain could easily have spread to neighboring Portugal.) Once the danger had passed, the bishops returned to Cova da Iria on May 13, 1938, and fulfilled their promise, performing a solemn ceremony of thanksgiving for what they explicitly acknowledged as a miraculous protection of their country by the Blessed Virgin. On that same occasion, they renewed the consecration of the Portuguese nation to the Immaculate Heart of Mary they had made seven years before. (See Neves, pp. 249-257.)

In recognition of the consecration by the Portuguese bishops, Our Lord promised a special protection to Portugal during World War II. He added that this protection would be a proof of the graces that would have been granted to the other nations if they likewise had been consecrated. (See Memoirs, pp. 436-438.)

However, the fact that Portugal was granted such graces in the thirties and forties did not mean that the communist danger and punishment by war would be definitively kept away from that country. This can be inferred from the subsequent passages of the cited letter, as well as from others found in *Memórias e Cartas da Irmã Lúcia* (see Memoirs, pp. 438, 440, 442), and from the visions of Jacinta that we set forth in chapter III of this work.

this reason, I deem it good to instill in people not only a great confidence in the mercy of our good Lord and in the protection of the Immaculate Heart of Mary, but also the awareness of the necessity of prayer accompanied by sacrifice, especially that which must be made in order to avoid sin." (See Memoirs, p. 426.)

In a letter dated December 2, 1940, Sister Lúcia addressed herself directly to Pope Pius XII in obedience to her spiritual directors, asking him to bestow his blessing upon the devotion of the first Saturdays and to extend its practice all over the world, adding:

"In 1929, during another apparition, Our Lady asked for the consecration of Russia to her Immaculate Heart, promising its conversion and to prevent the propagation of its errors by this means.... In several interior communications, Our Lord has not ceased to insist on this request, recently promising to shorten the days of tribulation with which He has determined to punish the nations for their crimes—through war, famine, and persecutions of Holy Church and Your Holiness—if Your Holiness deigns to consecrate the world to the Immaculate Heart of Mary, with special mention of Russia, and orders all the bishops of the world to do the same simultaneously in union with Your Holiness." (See Memoirs, p. 436; De Marchi, p. 312; Galamba de Oliveira, p. 153.)

On October 31, 1942, in a radio message to Portugal on the occasion of the closing of the jubilee year of the apparitions of Fátima, Pius XII consecrated the Church and the human race to the Immaculate Heart of Mary.

In 1943, Sister Lúcia had another revelation from Our Lord, which she related to Father Gonçalves in a letter dated May 4 of that same year.

"By order of His Excellency (the Most Reverend Manuel Maria Ferreira da Silva, titular bishop of Gurza), I had to communicate a brief message from Our Lord for the bishops here in Spain to the archbishop of Valladolid and another for the bishops of Portugal. Let us hope they all hear the voice of the good Lord. He wishes that the bishops of Spain gather in a retreat and draw up a plan of reform for the people, clergy, and religious orders. Because some convents!... And many members of others!... Do you understand? He wishes that it be made clear to souls that the true penance He now desires and demands is, before anything else, the sacrifice that each one must endeavor to make in order to fulfill his own religious and temporal duties. Because of the act of consecra-

The great apostle of Fátima, the Reverend Dr. Luis Fischer, examines the body of Jacinta at the first exhumation on September 12, 1935. The face of the seer was found to be incorrupt.

tion made by His Holiness, He promises that the war will end shortly. But since it was incomplete, the conversion of Russia will be postponed. If the bishops of Spain do not heed His wishes, it [Russia] will be once again the scourge with which God will punish them." (See Memoirs, p. 446.)

On July 7, 1952, in the Apostolic letter *Sacro Vergente Anno*, Pius XII consecrated the peoples of Russia to the Immaculate Heart of Mary in an apostolic letter.

At the Second Vatican Council, 510 archbishops and bishops from seventy-eight countries signed a petition entreating the vicar of Christ to consecrate the entire world—especially and explicitly Russia and the other nations dominated by communism—to the Immaculate Heart. The petition also requested that he order all the bishops of the Catholic world to join with him in this act on the same day. The document was presented personally to the Holy Father Pope Paul VI by the Most Reverend Geraldo de Proença Sigaud during a private audience on February 3, 1964. (See the complete text of the document in *Catolicismo*, no. 159, March 1964.)

Pope Paul VI, in closing the third session of Vatican II on November 21, 1964, "confided the human race" to the Immaculate Heart of Mary in the same act in which, to a standing ovation of the Council Fathers, he proclaimed Our Lady *"Mater Ecclesiae."* (See *Insegnamenti di Paoli VI*, vol. 2 [1964], p. 678.)

John Paul II made two consecrations of the world to the Immaculate Heart of Mary, one in Fátima on May 13, 1982, and the other in Rome on March 25, 1984. Both consecrations were preceded by the Pontiff's invitation to the bishops to unite with him in these acts. There is, however, no positive information to evaluate to what extent the bishops of the whole world carried out the consecration in union with the Pope, either in 1982 or in 1984. Moreover, Russia was not mentioned by name in either of these consecrations.

Consequently, Sister Lúcia always insisted until about mid-1989 that neither of these consecrations had been "valid" (taking the word in the sense of heeding the requirements Our Lady indicated to the seer). Since then, however, Sister Lúcia has been recognizing the validity of the consecration that John Paul II made on March 25, 1984.

Fátima experts are now divided over Sister Lúcia's position, some adhering to the new one and others preferring to hold to her former pronouncements.

The matter is too complex for us to resolve here. For the moment it is enough to note that on giving her view about a possible relation between the consecration and the spectacular events that occurred in Eastern Europe, mainly in the second semester of 1989, with the apparent collapse of communism—a relation that seems to be at the root of the change in the seer's position—*Sister Lúcia makes it clear that she is expressing a personal opinion and not transmitting a supernatural revelation.*

We are preparing a study of this interesting question to be brought out in due time.

*   *   *

It behooves us to pray with confidence that the unknown parts of the message entrusted to the seers be made known to the faithful, without any further delay, for the greater good of souls, for the defeat of the gnostic and egalitarian Revolution, and for the glorification of Mary Most Holy.

**Papal Legate Benedetto Cardinal Aloisi Masella solemnly crowns
the statue of Our Lady of Fátima in the presence of
800,000 pilgrims, May 13, 1946.**

**His Holiness Pope Pius XII addresses the Portuguese nation
on the occasion of the closing of the jubilee year
of the apparitions. October 31. 1942.**

Fátima:
Explanation and Cure for the
Contemporary Crisis

John R. Spann

Fátima: Explanation and Cure for the Contemporary Crisis

This commentary presupposes that the veracity of the Fátima apparitions has been demonstrated. In other words, we presume the reader acknowledges that Our Lady, and the Angel of Portugal before her, appeared to the three little shepherds and that the revelations made in the various apparitions have been faithfully reported by them. This, no doubt, could be ascertained employing the methods used in the study of any historical event of this type.

In Fátima, thousands of people have witnessed cures and prodigies that could be subjected to scientific analysis to verify their miraculous nature. In addition, the three shepherds were subjected to many interrogations, official and private, by both friends and enemies. These depositions could, in turn, undergo strict objective scrutiny that would take into account the shepherds' backgrounds, the life they led after the apparitions, and the pronouncements of the ecclesiastical authorities.

The great majority of the faithful believe in the apparitions and revelations of Fátima. Since this commentary is destined principally for Catholic readers, it seemed more beneficial to analyze some aspects of that which their souls, enlightened by the Faith, already accept, rather than to prove something they already hold to be true.

• The Great Upheavals of Our Times

Upon considering the turmoil of our century, two striking realities stand out.

1. The universal crisis. In the early part of this century, that is, until 1914, human society seemed to shine brilliantly. There was undeniable

progress in every field. Life had reached an unprecedented economic prosperity. Social life was easy and attractive. Humanity seemed to be heading for a golden era.

On the other hand, symptoms of deep trouble contrasted with this rosy picture. Both material and moral misery existed, but few people gave this matter the importance it warranted. Almost everyone expected that science and progress would put an end to all the problems. World War I came and shattered these expectations. In the war's aftermath, difficulties of all kinds steadily increased until 1939 when World War II broke out and ravaged the world for six years.

All this has brought us to the present situation, where it could be said that no country has remained unscathed by the grave crises that touch almost every aspect of life. Every nation is beset by agitation, disorder, the unrestraint of appetites and ambitions, the undermining of values, in short, if not by total anarchy, at least by a state of affairs that closely resembles it. And no statesman has yet come forth to offer a remedy in proportion to this morbid universal process.

2. The world wars. That of 1914-18 seemed to be an unsurpassable tragedy, but, in reality, that of 1939-45 exceeded it in length, compass, death toll, and the ruin left in its wake. The era of the Cold War kept us at the brink of a new world conflagration, which promised to be incalculably worse than any previous one. That era having passed with the fall of the Berlin Wall and the supposed demise of communism, mankind finds itself facing a world scene in many respects even more precarious. International and civil tensions and conflicts, any of which may explode, dot the globe as symptoms of a growing universal chaos that yet may bring the end of our civilization.

- **The Fátima Revelations:
  A Message for Today**

The essence of the messages of the Angel of Portugal and Our Lady is to open our eyes to the gravity of this situation, to explain it in light of the plans of Divine Providence, and to point out what is necessary in order to prevent the catastrophe. Our Lady is thus teaching us the history of our epoch and, more than this, its future.

The Roman Empire of the West closed with a catastrophe illuminated and analyzed by the genius of a great doctor, Saint Augustine. The wan-

The Basilica of Fátima
seen through one of the
arches of the colonnade.

ing of the Middle Ages was foreseen by the great prophet Saint Vincent Ferrer. The French Revolution was foreseen by another great prophet and teacher, Saint Louis de Montfort. But our times, which seem about to close with a new catastrophe, have an even greater privilege: Our Lady herself came to speak to us. Saint Augustine could only explain for posterity what caused the tragedy he witnessed. Saint Vincent Ferrer and Saint Louis de Montfort labored in vain to turn aside the tempests— men would not listen to them. Our Lady explained the reasons for the crisis and pointed out the remedy, predicting catastrophes if she were not heeded. From every viewpoint, by the nature of their content as well as the dignity of her who brought them, the revelations of Fátima surpass all other times when Providence has revealed to man the imminence of the great tempests of history.

The points of the Fátima revelation that concern this ominous approaching storm constitute the principal element of the message. The rest, no matter how important it may be, is a mere complement.

• The Moral Crisis

Of the six apparitions, there is not one in which the sins of humanity are not mentioned. They have become an unbearable weight in the scale of divine justice and are the ultimate cause of contemporary misery and disorder. Sins call down the just wrath of God, and because of them the most terrible chastisements threaten humanity. Men must convert if punishment is to be averted, and for men to convert the good must pray ardently for sinners and offer God many expiatory sacrifices.

• Prayer and Expiation for Sinners

In his message, the Angel of Portugal taught the little shepherds to ask for forgiveness for the evildoers and, moreover, to offer sacrifices for them. He especially mentioned the need to offer reparation to Our Lord in the Most Blessed Sacrament for the injuries He receives there, not only from those who profane Him but also from those who receive Him with indifference.

In her first apparition, Our Lady asked the shepherds to accept the laborious mission of expiating for sinners and foretold that they would have much to suffer. In the second apparition, she urged them to pray and sacrifice in order to lessen the number of souls who were being lost. To this end, she taught them a short prayer and showed them her Immaculate Heart crowned with thorns because of the sins being committed. In the third apparition, she showed them hell and the indescribable torments suffered by those cast there by the justice of God. She also insisted on the need of reparation for sin. In the fourth apparition, Our Lady taught another prayer of reparation and said that many souls are lost because there is no one to make reparation for them. In the fifth apparition, Our Lady moderated some excesses of the little shepherds in their ardor to make reparation, but she insisted that they needed to make sacrifices for sinners. She reiterated that men need to convert from their sins and cease tempting the justice of God to avert the chastisement.

Finally, in Tuy, Our Lady appeared to Sister Lúcia and said precisely the same thing. With this, we can see the constant theme behind all the apparitions: the world finds itself in the midst of a terrible religious and moral crisis; countless sins are being committed and are the true cause of universal desolation; the surest remedies for their effects are prayer and reparation.

- ## The Message of Fátima and
  ## the Voice of the Popes

The language of the popes has been essentially the same. Pius XI, for example, in the encyclical *Miserentissimus Redemptor* of May 8, 1928, affirmed that "the spectacle of contemporary misfortunes is so afflicting that in it can be seen the dawn of rising sorrows that will engender the man of sin who will rise up against everything that is called God and receive the honors of worship." He adds, "Truly, one cannot fail to think that the times predicted by Our Lord are near: 'and because iniquity hath abounded, the charity of many shall grow cold.'" Pius XII said that the agents who are demolishing Christian civilization, after having reached the height of their destructive action, are already building in this world the anti-Christian city. Its architect "has become more and more tangible with an amazing absence of scruples: first, Christ, yes; the Church, no! Afterward: God, yes; Christ, no! Finally, the impious shout: God is dead; even, God never existed! And, behold now the attempt to build the structure of the world on foundations that we do not hesitate to indicate as the causes principally responsible for the threat that weighs over humanity: economy without God, law without God, politics without God. The 'enemy' labored and labors so that Christ may become a stranger in the university, in the school, in the family, in the administration of justice, in the making of laws, in the governing of nations, and in the decisions that determine war and peace everywhere. At present, he uses the press to corrupt the world and films to murder the modesty of young men and women and destroy the love between spouses; he inculcates a nationalism that leads to war" (Allocution to the men of Italian Catholic Action, October 12, 1952, *Discorsi e Radiomessaggi*, vol. XIV, p. 359).

• The Message of Fátima and False Optimism

We are well aware that these words of wise realism contrast with a certain widespread tendency among the Catholics of the West. Out of a spirit of accommodation and opportunism, out of a puerile desire to conform to the events of this century and usher it down tortuous paths to a chimerical conversion, for several decades countless Catholics have thought and acted in this world of crisis and ruin as if they lived in more blessed times—such as the thirteenth century with Saint Louis IX reigning in France, Saint Ferdinand III in Castile, and Saint Thomas Aquinas and Saint Bonaventure illuminating the Church with the splendor of their knowledge and virtue. Although this carefree attitude is usually found among the young, unaware of the evident gravity of the present crisis, these Catholics, often in their forties or older, frantically joined the laughter and levity, praising a state of affairs that wrings anguished groans and even wails of sorrow from others. And if anyone tried to open their eyes, their indifferent hearts became furious. Seemingly tolerant of everything and everyone, they could not bear to face the gravity of the situation.

Were the words of Our Lady and the popes enough to convince them? Apparently not.

• The Message of Fátima and Nearsighted Catholics

Along with this feverish optimism that would make Catholic life an unending party where no one matures, an eternal picnic that disdains everything pious and evocative of sorrow, a world that abhors the crucifix with the divine Victim's wounds shedding redeeming blood and the black vestments for the Mass of the Dead, and so forth, we have another defect to consider: apathy.

There exists a false piety that has causes men to avoid consideration of all the great problems: Is Christian civilization in dissolution? Is the world crumbling? Is the earth in upheaval? He who is intoxicated by this form of piety sees nothing, feels nothing, notices nothing. His life is merely a petty one, lived in the upright, peaceful fulfillment of his petty personal duties, in his petty acts of piety, in solving only his petty problems of conscience. His zeal goes no farther than his horizons, which, it is painful to say, go little farther than the tip of his nose. If you talk to him about politics, sociology, the philosophy and theology of history, or apologetics, he changes the subject with a certain fear, the fear termites have of daylight. For this man also, Fátima has a great lesson.

Our Lady came to earth to excite the zeal of souls to this immense panorama of today's crisis. She wants piety, she wants reparation, but the reason for her desire is God's interest in this vast world. What is at issue within the limitless perspectives of Fátima is not the salvation of this or that soul considered individually, but something higher with a wider scope. It is the salvation of all mankind that must be fought for, because it is not any particular person, but countless souls that risk being lost in one of the gravest crises of history. And it is to this immense task that Our Lady calls not just one Simon of Cyrene, but many, multitudes, even legions of them.

Fátima was not just an appeal for three shepherd children to do penance. This appeal was directed at the whole world. The piety of contemporary man must have, so to speak, a strong expiatory and reparatory note.

- **The Message of Fátima and the "Heresy of Good Works"**

Let us consider another point. No one can question the importance of action. The popes daily call the faithful to it. However, in essence, Fátima says nothing in particular about it. Does Divine Providence judge it unnecessary or of no urgency? Who could condone such an aberration? Why, then, does Fátima appear oblivious to it? It is because we live in an epoch that is dominated by the senses, an epoch in which the need to act is easily understood, for action is something perceived by the senses, whose value can often be translated into figures and statistics and is visible in a palpable form. For this reason, it is not that difficult to call the attention of truly zealous souls to the importance of action. But it has always been very difficult to attract souls to what is spiritual, interior, invisible. Thus, it is harder for man to comprehend prayer and the interior life, and he consequently dedicates less time and interest to them. It is quite understandable that Our Lady of Fátima insisted on the necessity of prayer and penance to the point of making it the essential element of her message. How Dom Chautard, author of the treatise on the interior life *The Soul of the Apostolate*—who spoke of the "heresy" of attempting to lead a life of action, of good works, without an interior life, which is necessary as a vivifying source for the active life—would have profited from this fact if, at his time, this topic had been as clear as it is today!

• Prayer Alone Is Not Enough: Atonement Is Necessary

We come to a last essential point. Our Lady did not speak only of prayer. She wants expiation, sacrifice. Has any other epoch tried harder to avoid suffering? Has any other epoch spoken less of the need for mortification? Has any other epoch had a weaker notion of the importance of sacrifice? It is precisely to this point that Our Lady wanted to attract our special attention. During the great centuries of piety, expiation was commonplace in the life of men and nations. Great pilgrimages were undertaken to atone for sins. In caves, forests, and cloisters could be found veritable legions of souls dedicated to lives of expiation. Wills were drawn up leaving entire fortunes to pious works of charity for the remission of sins. There were confraternities wholly turned toward inspiring penance. There were processions of atonement in which entire cities took part. Today there are still collective manifestations of piety, but no matter how much the Church may call us to penance, what role does penance play in such manifestations? What role does it play in our private lives? A small one, very small indeed. It seems indisputable that Fátima also teaches us a valuable lesson on this point.

- ## The Message of Fátima and the Crisis in the Church

The message brought to us in 1917 by Our Lady of Fátima is widely known: If humanity does not turn aside from the ways of sin, the world will suffer a frightful chastisement, and the instrument of that chastisement will be the errors of Russia, as we have previously seen.

The message of Fátima has been communicated to practically the whole world and especially to Catholic peoples. Books in many languages, some of them best sellers, newspapers, and radio and television stations that have reported extensively on the main events related to the apparitions at Cova da Iria constitute what is perhaps an unparalleled coverage, making Fátima one of the best-known events of our times.

In this worldwide effort, special emphasis should be given to the role played by the pilgrim statues carved under the guidance of Sister Lúcia that travelled around the globe in the forties and fifties, stimulating awareness of the message of Fátima. Thus, at the time of Pius XII, a most worthy design of the Church hierarchy to make the will of Our Lady known to all men was begun.

Nevertheless, those were times already foreshadowing the spiritual catastrophes brought on by the progressivism of our days and referred to by Paul VI in his historical allocution of December 7, 1968, to the Lombard Seminary, when he noted that the Church was undergoing a mysterious process of "self-destruction."

Consequently, preaching about Fátima should have had a fundamentally anticommunist tone and denounced the errors and deviations of contemporary society—errors that drag men into communism by way of punishment. This preaching should have promoted the devotion to the Immaculate Heart of Mary and the fulfillment of Our Lady's requests as the solution to the unprecedented crisis of the contemporary world. In most cases, this was done weakly and ineffectively.

Because of this, the devotion to Our Lady of Fátima has not yet achieved its original purpose, despite the fact that it has spread widely. Merely praising Our Lady of Fátima, as one would praise the Mother of God under any of her other invocations, is, of course, something very praiseworthy and desirable, as would be any other act of devotion to the Blessed Virgin; but it lacks that special liaison to the present historical hour and to the designs of Our Lady in relation to the message of Fátima.

From this point of view, devotion to Our Lady of Fátima should have been much more emphasized in our times than the many other excellent devotions the Holy Ghost has inspired in times past. But this has not happened. Undoubtedly, the movement of piety occasioned by Fátima has done much good—but not all the good one could have hoped for. Objectivity demands that we recognize that the goal established by Our Lady in Fátima has not been reached and that the conditions set down by her to prevent the chastisement have not been met.

• What Devotion to Our Lady of Fátima Specifically Entails

The authors who write about Fátima stress that in Our Lady's first appearance she had an expression that was "neither sad nor happy, but serious," with an air of mild reproach. This expression conforms perfectly to the seriousness of the message she brought. In the third apparition (in which she revealed the secret to the seers), Our Lady began to reveal the sadness in her soul. Finally, in the last apparition, she said men "must amend their lives and ask forgiveness for their sins." And with an even sadder expression, she said, "Let them offend Our Lord no more, for He is already much offended."

This should be our state of mind in order to perceive the true meaning of the message of Fátima. Our Lady wants us to share her seriousness in face of the calamitous state of the world. She wants us to share her sadness at the sins of the world and her apprehension over the chastisements that will fall upon humanity. If our souls are so disposed, she will care for our spiritual and material necessities as a reward.

When Our Lady unfurled these vast panoramas before Lúcia, Francisco, and Jacinta, telling them that the world would suffer catastrophes, that the errors of Russia would spread throughout the world, and that several nations would be annihilated, it is difficult to imagine that the seers were concerned only with their own spiritual or material problems. Rather, we can only envision them paying close attention to what the Mother of God was saying and being moved by these words. In fact,

The Fátima square during one of the feast days.
Pilgrims approach the basilica on their knees in a spirit of penance.

the spiritual fruits they reaped came as a consequence of sharing Our Lady's concerns.

Each one of us should do likewise. If the Mother of God is saddened and weeps at the situation of the world, we should also be moved and make the resolution to work seriously to stop those tears. The rest shall be added unto us, for the Blessed Virgin, the Mother of Mercy, will not fail to provide for our souls and necessities—even the material ones. But this she will do only on the condition that we obediently and faithfully fulfill her requests.

This is the heart of the devotion to Our Lady of Fátima and the theme proper to our prayers and thoughts at all times.

- **Our Lady of Fátima: Our Lady of the Counter-Revolution**

In Fátima, the Mother of the Redeemer denounced the sins of humanity that would lead the world to succumb to Russia's errors. What sins were these?

In his celebrated study *Revolution and Counter-Revolution*, Professor Plinio Corrêa de Oliveira describes the centuries-old revolutionary process which, erupting in the Renaissance and Protestantism at the end of the Middle Ages and passing through the bloody stage of the French Revolution, resulted in this century's communist revolution and its present metamorphosis.

But what form has the revolutionary process adopted today on the international scene? It is accelerating its advance on all fronts: in the ubiquity of socialist and communist errors (the disintegration of the Soviet bloc notwithstanding), in the waves of immoral fashions (about which Our Lady spoke to Jacinta in apparitions after 1917), in the entire cultural or tendential revolution (see *Revolution and Counter-Revolution*, pp. 26, 142), in the process of "self-destruction" afflicting the Mystical Body of Christ, and so on.

If Our Lady pointed to communism as the result of humanity's sinful state, she was obviously referring to a process of rebellion against God, which is expounded in Professor Corrêa de Oliveira's cited work. She thus teaches us to execrate that process and wants us to dedicate all our efforts and means to repel whatever leads to communism. In a word,

Our Lady invites us to fight for the Counter-Revolution, the process of restoring the order destroyed by the Revolution.

Thus, the mediatrix of all graces calls us to this particular form of the love of God in which we grow in awareness of the interests of the Holy Catholic Church and Christian civilization and make them triumphant through the Counter-Revolution and the establishment of her reign. This is what Our Lady herself promised at Fátima: "Finally, my Immaculate Heart will triumph."

Our Lady of Fátima can thus with every right be called "Our Lady of the Counter-Revolution."

- **The Probable Content of the Third Part of the Secret: The Crisis in the Church**

We shall now deal with the famous secret of Fátima, revealed to the seers in the July apparition.

The secret is composed of three parts, the first two of which were revealed by Sister Lúcia in 1941. The third part, which the Holy See has not yet decided to divulge, still holds the world in suspense about the message of Fátima.

In the second part of the secret, the Mother of God said that a chastisement would come. This punishment, which would especially afflict temporal society because of its march toward communism, would be so terrible that entire nations would disappear. It is difficult to believe that Our Lady would warn man of this hecatomb in the civil order and yet not warn him of a much worse tragedy—the crisis in the Church.

It is comprehensible that a pious soul would quake at such a hypothesis before it became self-evident. But once public, it must be seen, recognized, and accepted; it cannot be avoided. Given the lukewarm reception most Catholics gave the message of Fátima, let alone the formal rejection of it by significant sectors of them and the appalling connivance of so many clergymen and laymen with communism, how could all this not deserve special mention in the secret of Fátima?

It is natural that such a dramatic prospect should have been kept secret due to the climate inside the Church in 1917. The presence of Saint Pius X could still be felt not only in the memory of his recent death, but in the incorruptness of his body. Communism was about to seize power in Russia. A reaction against the revolutionary process was still possible. In spite of problems, there was far more composure and decorum in the Church than there is today. At that time, a prediction of the panorama we have before us could have shaken innumerable souls. But from the moment this evil could be readily confirmed by almost daily experience, the proclamation of its existence would only serve to confirm souls in the Faith.

If this is, in fact, as we conjecture, the content of the third part of the secret, it is perfectly understandable that Our Lady communicated it to the seers to be revealed at the right moment.

Sister Lúcia was left on earth by Our Lady in order to fulfill a certain mission. It would be normal to assume that, due to the chaos in society and the crisis in the Church, her mission includes attesting to the veracity of the third part of the secret when it is finally told to the world in order to prevent confusion, doubt, and rejection among the faithful.

Respectful of the legitimate decision of the ecclesiastical authorities to withhold the secret's revelation, there is nothing, nonetheless, that impedes us from lifting our hearts to the throne of the Blessed Virgin to paraphrase the prophet Samuel, crying, *"Loquere, Domina, quia audit servus tuus"* (1 Kings 3:10). Speak, O Lady, by the mouth of Sister Lúcia, so that thy true message can be heard with certainty and move the hearts of the just.

Bibliography

Ayres da Fonseca, S.J., Rev. Luiz Gonzaga. *Nossa Senhora de Fátima.* 5th ed. Petrópolis, Brazil: Editora Vozes, 1954.

Chautard, O.C.S.O., Dom Jean-Baptiste. *The Soul of the Apostolate.* Trappist, Kentucky: Abbey of Gethsemani, 1946.

Corrêa de Oliveira, Plinio. *Revolution and Counter-Revolution.* 3d ed. York Penn.: The American Society for the Defense of Tradition, Family and Property (TFP), 1993.

De Marchi, I.M.C., Rev. John. *Era uma Senhora mais brilhante que o sol....* 3d ed. Cova da Iria, Portugal: Seminário das Missões de N. Sra. de Fátima.

——. *The Crusade of Fátima: the Lady More Brilliant than the Sun.* 3d printing. Adapted by Fathers Asdrubal Castello Branco and Philip C. M. Kelly, C.S.C. New York: P.J. Kenedy & Sons, 1948. Except where otherwise stated, references are from the Portuguese edition.

De Montfort, Saint Louis-Marie Grignion. *True Devotion to the Blessed Virgin.* 5th ed. New York: P.J. Kenedy & Sons, 1909.

Fazenda, S.J., Rev. Antonio de Almeida. *Meditações dos primeiros sábados.* 2d ed. Braga, Portugal: Mensageiro do Coração de Jesus, 1953.

Galamba de Oliveira, Most Rev. José. "História das Aparições." In *Fátima, Altar do Mundo,* vol. II, pp. 21-160. Porto, Portugal: Ocidental Editora, 1954.

Mariz, S.J., Rev. Luiz Gonzaga. *Fátima, onde o céu tocou a terra.* 2d ed. Salvador, Brazil: Editora Mensageiro da Fé, 1954.

Memórias e Cartas da Irmã Lúcia. Introduction, English translation, and notes by Father Antonio Maria Martins. Porto, Portugal: Simão Guimarães, Filhos, 1973. Facsimile edition of the manuscripts of Sister Lúcia. Portuguese text also in type, with English and French translations included. Two other editions were made of the Portu-guese text, one in Brazil (*O Segredo de Fátima nas memórias e car-tas da Irmã Lúcia*, Edições Loyola, São Paulo, 1974), and the other in Portugal (*O Segredo de Fátima e o futuro de Portugal nos escritos da Irmã Lúcia*, L.E., Porto, 1974). Except where otherwise stated, references are from the facsimile edition.

Neves, Rev. Moreira das. "As grandes jornadas de Fátima." In *Fátima, Altar do Mundo*, vol. II, pp. 205-303. Porto, Portugal: Ocidental Edi-tora, 1954.

Reis, Rev. Sebastião Martins dos. *A Vidente de Fátima dialoga e re-sponde pelas Aparições*. Braga, Portugal: Tip. Editorial Franciscana, 1970.

⎯⎯⎯. *Síntese crítica de Fátima: Incidências e Repercussões*. Évora, Portugal: Edição do Autor, 1967.

Rendeiro, O.P., Friar Francisco. "A consagração pela Igreja do culto de Nossa Senhora de Fátima." In *Fátima, Altar do Mundo*, vol. II, pp. 163-198. Porto, Portugal: Ocidental Editora, 1954.

Walsh, William Thomas. *Our Lady of Fátima*. 4th printing. New York: The Macmillan Company, 1947.

⎯⎯⎯. *Nossa Senhora de Fátima*. 2d ed. São Paulo, Brazil: Edições Melhoramentos, 1949. Except where otherwise stated, references to Walsh are from the Portuguese edition.

The *America Needs Fatima* campaign has an inspiring selection of devotion-building materials for adults and children.

For more copies of *Fatima: Prophecies of Tragedy or Hope?* or for a complete listing of other titles, please call **1-717-225-7147** or write to:

America Needs Fatima
P.O. Box 1868
York, PA 17405